Dr. Jignesh Shah's

UTSAV

'The Celebration of Life'

Nexus Stories Publication
Bhārata

NEXUS STORIES PUBLICATION®

Surat, Gujarat, India.

Title – UTSAV 'The Celebration of Life'

First Published by Nexus Stories Publication 2023

Copyright © Dr. Jignesh Shah 2023

All Rights Reserved.

ISBN # 978-81-19178-97-1

This book has been published with all efforts taken to make the material error-free after the consent of the author. However, the author and the publisher do not assume and hereby disclaim any liability to any party for any loss, damage, or disruption caused by errors or omissions, whether such errors or omissions result from negligence, accident, or any other cause.

No part of this book may be used or reproduced in any manner whatsoever without written permission from the author/publisher, except in the case of brief quotations embodied in critical articles and reviews.

Declaration: This book's content is owned by the author/editor. Nexus Stories Publication™ is a service provider for book design/distribution.

Disclaimer (From the Author): The views, ideas, thoughts and opinions expressed by the author and names of people, names of organizations, places, events and incidents mentioned in this book by the author purely aims to spread awareness and enlighten the readers at large. There is no intention to hurt anybody's sentiments or malign anybody's image.

Publication

Nexus Stories Publication™, Surat (Gujarat), Bhārata

www.nexus-stories.com # +91 87800 80718 # www.nexus-stories.in

Shri Krishnam Vande Jagadguru

"Watch your thoughts; they become words.
Watch your words; they become actions.
Watch your actions; they become habits.
Watch your habits; they become character.
Watch your character; it becomes your destiny."

In the loving memory of my Mother

<u>Late Smt Sarojben Shah</u>

Preface

A judicious blend of multiple resources is the key to the effective functioning of organizations across the globe and of all these resources, one of the most important resources is Human resource. Human Resource is the foundation to build a strong organization as it is the only asset that appreciates over a period of time. Organizations, in the current scenario, are investing a lot on human resources as they understand that effective management as well as development of human resources plays a pivotal role in the success of any organization. A dedicated, committed, passionate, efficient and effective human resource is a key to the productivity as well as profitability of the organization.

In the above mentioned context, Being extremely passionate about the HR profession and with a purpose of giving back to society, I would like to celebrate my life with all of you as I enter into my 60th glorious year. The best way to celebrate this momentous occasion was to present all of you with the compilation of some of the magnificent, worthy, admirable, challenging, arduous and demanding chapters of my life. I have always showcased courage, strength and stability in whatever situation life has thrown at me and have always believed that whether it was a Peak or Valley, it was all meant to be celebrated. My philosophy of celebrating success as well as failures have been instrumental in getting me to the stage where I am today and thus The compilation of my life story has been named - **"Utsav - The celebration of Life"**

This book talks about my experience in managing and developing Human Resources across a tenure of more than three decades. It aims to serve as an ultimate guide to blossoming HR professionals, budding entrepreneurs and will help every corporate person understand the essence of HR in personal as well as professional context.

The book is divided into eight parts with each part discussing different aspects of my personal as well as professional life. Part 1 titled "The Beginning" talks about my early life and education, Part 2 titled "HR Voyage" talks about my experience in different organizations with the detailed discussion about the experience in each organization and the unique HR initiatives taken by me during my career, Part 3 titled "The path to wisdom" talks about pearls of wisdom that I have derived from my HR voyage in different organizations and various interesting and mesmerizing stories depicting various life lessons. Part 4 titled - "The Spiritual Journey" talks about my inclination towards spirituality, the importance of Yoga and Meditation for one's physical, mental and emotional wellbeing and Learnings from Srimad Bhagavad Gita. Part 5 Titled "The Traits and Value System" talks about my personality traits and the core values that have been an integral part of my personal as well as professional life. Part 6 titled – "Way Forward" talks about my future plans, Part 7 – titled "Conclusion" summarizes my entire journey and Part 8 – titled "A Kaleidoscope of Milestones" talks about my accolades and achievements across the tenure

I am very sure that my personal as well as professional experiences shared in this book will be a great value addition to the readers and help them embark on the path of progress and prosperity there by enriching their life journey.

I feel fortunate to have had the opportunity to fulfill my dream of sharing my experience, knowledge and wisdom and doing my bit by giving back to society.

I invite you all for this Grand Utsav.

Happy Reading............

Dr Jignesh shah

Date: 07.12.2023

*****

Foreword

Multiple books have been written on the subject mentioned in the preface of the book. But there are some books that stand the test of time and remain **"Must Read". "Utsav - The Celebration of Life",** authored by Dr Jignesh Shah, is one such book.

My association with Dr Jignesh Shah goes back to 1992. I have seen him rise through various odds and add tremendous value to all the associated organizations. He has always amazed me with his passion and dedication towards the profession of HR. His pursuit towards excellence and a never-ending zeal and enthusiasm to learn new things is something that has helped him make a mark in the HR fraternity. Facing challenges with a smiling face and a positive attitude is a trait that has added to his success in both personal as well as professional front. In his celebrated career of more than three decades, I have always seen him striving and working hard to enrich the lives of budding professionals and help them attain physical, mental and emotional wellbeing.

If you are passionate about HR and are looking forward to understanding the nuances of this profession, start digging in this book. His life journey depicted in the book which encompasses his early life, professional as well as personal experiences, accolades and achievements and spiritual journey have added enormous value to the book and will help all of you understand the narrative in a simple manner. The book is so easy and enjoyable that I found myself drawn to the book instantly and I am very confident that just like me, once you start reading the book you will be completely engrossed in the content and will not put it aside until you have reached the crispness of the final page.

My heartfelt wishes to Dr Jignesh Shah for this amazing effort towards compilation of his life journey and presenting the same in such an enlightening and educative manner.

Manish Baraiya

Date 07.12.2023

*****

Acknowledgments

I take this opportunity to thank certain people whose support has made a difference to this text and made this book possible.

My Wife - Ms Nimisha Shah - For standing by me while I chase my dreams and for her unwavering support in all the activities that I have undertaken.

Ms Shalini Vaid - For collecting my thoughts and articulating the same in chapters.

Shri Rajubhai Pathak and family and particularly Mr Brij Pathak - For being a constant source of motivation and encouragement towards compilation of this wonderful piece of work

My Son and Daughter in Law - Dr Yash Shah and Dr Margi Shah - For being my biggest cheerleaders and for their unconditional love and support in all my endeavours.

My well-wishers - For sending me positivity and always being a part of my happiness.

*****

About the Author

Dr. Jignesh Shah is currently Chief Human Resource Officer at RKC Infrabuilt Pvt. Ltd. An HR icon who has excelled in establishing innovative HR systems and institutionalizing a strong performance-driven culture across various organizations. Born in a town named Padra-Baroda, he received a Master's Degree in Social work (MSW) and Post Graduate Diploma in Industrial relations and Personnel Management from M S University, Baroda. He also holds an MBA - in HR from Newport University - USA and has been awarded Doctorate in Organizational Leadership. In his illustrious HR career of more than three decades, Dr. Jignesh Shah has worked with some of the top Engineering, Pharma, Petrochemical, Polyester, FMCG, Power, and Infrastructure com panies. He has been sharing his knowledge in the field of HR by serving as a Guest faculty, Guest speaker as well and Panellist to various reputed B Schools, Universities as well and Management Associations. Having worked with a multi-generational workforce, Dr Jignesh Shah has witnessed the transition of the HR function from a personnel department to a progressive HR department. His passion for the HR profession, eagerness to learn new things, and an attitude of embracing and accepting change positively helped him ride this transition wholeheartedly and with sheer excellence. With a strong understanding of business, Dr Jignesh Shah is skilled in designing and developing various avenues of managing human resources which includes Strategic Manpower Planning, Recruitment and Selection, HR Policies and Practices, Competency Mapping, Compensation and Reward Systems, Performance Management, Training and Development, Labour Compliances, Employee Counseling and Wellness, Employee Engagement, Capacity Building and Succession Planning, Grievance Redressal and Union Negotiations. His exemplary contribution in the field of HR has lead Dr Jignesh Shah earn multiple accolades. Some of these include Most Influencing HR Leader in India, Best Innovation in HR, Best Employee Engagement Professional, Best CHRO. He has also succeeded in registering his name amongst 100 HR super achievers and Asia's 100 Powerful HR leaders. Dr Jignesh Shah is also a certified Multistyle Yoga teacher. **"An uninterrupted working atmosphere"** is what he considers to be his ultimate Forte.

Dr. Jignesh Shah

Date: 07.12.2023

*****

About the Editor

Dr Himani Sheth

Dr Himani Sheth is a passionate HR professional with over 18 years of experience in the field of HR which includes 13 years in Teaching and Research and 5 years in Industry. Currently, she is working at the School of Management Studies, LJ University. She has been awarded a Doctorate degree in HR and holds an MBA degree with specialization in HR and an M Com degree with specialization in Costing. Her forte includes imparting knowledge on Human Resource Management, Change Management, Human Resource Development, Strategic Human Resource Management, Compensation Management and Organizational Behaviour. She is skilled in imparting knowledge and developing material on practicalities involved in managing human resources and analysing human behaviour in organizations. She has served as a Guest / Visiting faculty at various renowned as well as reputed institutions like B K School of Professional and Management Studies - Department of Management Studies, B K School of Professional and Management Studies - Department of Maritime Management, Amrut Mody School of Management, Ahmedabad Management Association, Shanti Business School. Her research work has been published in various national and international journals. She has been recognized multiple times for excellence in teaching as well as research.

Dr Himani Sheth

Date: 07.12.2023

*****

Contents

"If Wealth is lost

Nothing is lost

If Health is lost

Something is lost

If Character is lost

Every thing is lost."

1 : The Beginning

1.1   Parents and Early Life

I was born in a middle-class family in 1964. During this period my family was staying in a town named Padra, in the city of Baroda. My father was working with the Indian Air Force and thus had a transferable job. My mother was a homemaker. My education was of primary importance to my parents and hence they decided that I will be staying with my uncle in Padra and they will be moving to different locations thereby ensuring that my primary education is completed smoothly under the guidance of my uncle.

1.2   Educational Overview

Being always a bright student and scoring distinction across my academic career, I completed my primary education in Padra and then moved to Baroda City to pursue high school education. After completing my high school education, I took admission in M S University, Baroda for graduation and decided to specialize in commerce stream.

The road to higher education

After completing the graduation course from M S University, Baroda, I got two job offers. One was from LIC and the other one was at the collector's office designated as clerk with a salary offer of Rs 2500 per month. Not following my father's wish of accepting the job offer and getting settled in life, with no help from him, I decided to pursue higher education to build a professional career which I always dreamt of and to fulfill the dream I started work part time at a salary of Rs 1000 per month. The amount of Rs 1000 was enough to cover my routine expenses and pay fees for higher studies which included MSW, LLB, PGDIRPM and a specialized course in Hospitality Management.

Earning the MSW degree

While I decided to reject both the jobs offered to me after commerce graduation, in the process of pursuing my dream of higher education, my teacher encouraged me to take up the course of Chartered Accountancy and helped me gain practical exposure in accounting by providing me a chance to work in his office. But somehow I was not inclined towards accountancy and so decided to take up a course named MSW at M S University, Baroda. Securing a job of labour welfare officer and the placement records post completion of this course, attracted me to pursue the course. It was mandatory to appear for a written test in order to get admission in the MSW course and thus I appeared for one. Post the written test, Baroda witnessed riots and thus curfew was levied in my residential area and so I could not go and check the result. During those days, my teacher for whom I was working called me for urgent work and suggested that I leave at midnight from my residence to avoid curfew restrictions and reach his residence which was not under curfew. I took the risk and left my home at midnight to address the urgency of my teacher. Next day while passing through the M S University, Baroda, I thought about checking the result and was glad to find out that I had cleared the exam. The process of admission also involved appearing for a group discussion and viva but by the time I got to know about the written test result, the group discussion process was over. I met the Dean and explained to him the reason for my absence from the group discussion and considering the same, the Dean told me to write the same narration on a piece of paper. On submission of the same, the Dean decided to hold a staff meeting the next day and asked me to remain present in case I am required to be a part of the staff meeting. The staff meeting lasted for three long hours and it was concluded that if I pass the viva I will be admitted to the course. I would like to emphasize the fact that this was the turning point of my life.

*****

2 : HR Voyage

2.1   Experience with various organizations

Episode 1 - Zaverichand Gaekwad Ltd

In the year 1990, after completing MSW, I was selected by a company called Zaverichand Gaekwad to be offered the designation of a Trainee - Personnel. A challenging situation occurred on the fourth day of my very first assignment. I was all alone and was assigned a task of handling a factory inspection visit which was led by a senior government officer. In accordance with my strong personality, I handled the same with utmost diligence. I greeted him and extended all the required hospitality for him. During my conversation with him, I gave him my introduction and told him that I was a MSW graduate fresher having spent only 4 days in the organization and thus don't have much idea about the compliance levels at the factory. The senior government officer appreciated my honesty and conveyed that since none of the senior person was available at the factory he does not want to make any remarks which may go against the organization and put me in trouble. He further instructed me to visit his office after 4 days with all the documents mentioned in the list handed over to me. After an hour of interaction he left the factory. The next day, I reported the incident to the HOD and shared my first experience of handling a senior government officer. The HOD too was impressed by the same and subsequently both of us visited the senior government officer's office and furnished the required documents and were glad to know that there were no adverse remarks made against the organization.

Take away for HR Buddy

Giving importance and due respect to the government officials is very important. It is not necessary to fulfill all their demands but you need to provide them all the necessary comfort and hospitality and give a patient listening to them. While dealing with them an employee needs to be honest and transparent to win their trust. This will help them to manage the situation in a balanced manner.

Episode 2 - Jyoti Ltd

While pursuing a post graduate diploma in Industrial Relations and personnel management, an evening course, I met a lot of working professionals and came to know about an opening at Jyoti Ltd, Baroda. I appeared for the interview and got selected for their switchgear plant in Gorwa, Baroda and was fortunate enough to handle a rich profile and get experience and exposure of dealing with Industrial relations issues in the context of multiplicity of unions.

In connection to the same, I will share a very interesting incident. At Jyoti Ltd, we decided to make Identity Cards for all the employees with their photographs. All the employees were communicated the same and were asked to come in appropriate and neat dressing as their photographs were supposed to be clicked. The whole exercise was planned very smoothly and as mentioned above all the employees were informed about the same well in advance. I was at a junior level at that point of time and so one of the employees decided to tease me or may be test me during this exercise. One of the secretaries of the union had come to get his photograph clicked along with his colleagues. When the photographer asked him to come for the click, he removed his shirt and wore it as a turban on his head and then asked the photographer to click the photograph. The photographer was not comfortable with this behaviour and reported about this incident to me. I immediately rushed to the site and requested the secretary to behave according to the company norms and not create a scene about the same. I convinced him multiple times to remove the shirt tied as a turban on his head and wear it properly and get the photograph clicked. In Spite of my continuous, consistent and multiple requests, the secretary was adamant to not wear the shirt and continue this behaviour. So I decided to allow him to do this and told the photographer to click his photograph without the shirt and with a turban tied on his head. The photographer followed my instructions and clicked his photograph. This came as a shocker for the secretary as he had never expected I would do this. He got furious about this and asked me why I did that. My simple reply was that "In Spite of my continuous efforts you did not agree to what I said and You had told me to do whatever I wanted and I did it".So once the photograph was taken, I took the roll from the photographer and reported the incident to the plant manager. The plant manager then reported the incident to the CEO and then the CEO called me and the plant manager for a joint meeting. We narrated the whole incident to the CEO and it was decided to take action against this employee on the grounds of indiscipline. The CEO called the IR Head and informed him about this incident and instructed him to issue a show cause notice against the worker. As the information percolated in the organization, the secretary along with his colleagues were very upset and angry as they did not expect that this issue would be taken to such a high level. Meanwhile, the very next day, a show cause notice was issued to the secretary and he was asked to give an explanation for his behaviour. Further, as the explanation was not satisfactory, a charge sheet was issued and a domestic inquiry was conducted. Being the main witness, I presented the facts with evidence during the domestic inquiry. The charges against the secretary were proved beyond doubt. The secretary was now a bit uncomfortable and decided to find a solution for the raised situation. He requested the management to provide him a safe passage and not dismiss him, suspend him or take any other punitive action against him. The parties involved decided to come to a solution and the matter was addressed by issuing a warning letter.

Take away for the HR Buddy

In Spite of being at a Junior Level, one should always have clarity about the work and courage to handle any situation especially while dealing with the blue - collar workers. If you are honest towards your duty and can stand for the truth, no force can stop you from fulfilling your task. Be courageous irrespective of the hierarchy that you belong to.

Episode 3 - Lupin Laboratories Ltd

Absenteeism of workers was one of the major issues at Lupin Laboratories Ltd. It was very important to bring absenteeism down without creating any disturbance in the working atmosphere of the organization. An overnight decision or an unplanned action would have resulted in a chaotic situation which would have led to multiple issues disturbing the overall functioning of the organization. It was necessary to plan and strategize a suitable action to tackle this problem and bring a solution to the same. Me along with my team decided to solve this issue with utmost planning as well as patience. The HR department along with the senior management decided to review the absenteeism data of the workers every quarter and made a SOP to handle the issue. As a part of the SOP, the first step was counseling of the absentee. The absentee was called on for counseling which was conducted in the presence of senior management. The counseling aimed at making the worker understand the loss that would occur to him personally as well as to the departments due to absenteeism. The counseling was not at all directed towards any intention of punishing the worker or penalizing him. The worker was very clearly informed that he will be provided all the possible support in case of genuine reasons / medical emergency. The whole discussion was documented and validated by official signatures by the worker, HR official as well as the senior management representative. A copy of the same was given to the worker also. In case there is no improvement in the absenteeism record of that particular worker in the next quarter, then the second step was to issue an advisory letter to that worker where the absenteeism was put on record. If the same thing continues in the next quarter as well then the third step was to issue a show cause notice to the worker asking him for an explanation on his absenteeism. There can be two things in this case. Either the explanation is not satisfactory or either it is satisfactory. In case the explanation is not satisfactory then in accordance with the model standing orders a charge sheet is issued against the worker and a domestic inquiry is conducted where based on the submission of records it is decided whether the charges are proved or not based on the report from the inquiry officer. Once the report is received from the inquiry officer that the charges are proved then as a first step a warning letter is issued to the worker and the same thing is followed in case the explanation of the worker is genuine. If the same indiscipline continued then the warning letter was followed by 1 day suspension, 2 day suspension, 3 day suspension, 4 day suspension, stoppage of annual increment, demotion and termination. Meanwhile, we also visited the residence colony of the workers to understand their family background and lifestyle and the reasons behind their absenteeism and with this approach there were a lot of things that came up about the lifestyle of the workers which included liquor issues, involvement in illegal activities like gambling and related issues. And so simultaneously we initiated a necessary corrective approach to help them come out of these addictions. With all these strategies, ways and means mentioned above and consistent and dedicated efforts of three years, we succeeded in bringing down the absenteeism rate to 2 % from 10 %.

Take away for HR Buddy

Rather than taking hasty actions, you should prepare systematic strategies with departmental support as well as support from the top management. It will always prove to be fruitful as it will create a reasonable amount of scope for employees to understand their mistakes and take corrective actions and will also refrain them from making further mistakes.

Episode 4 - Lupin Laboratories Ltd

I always believe that HR is truly understood when one is on the floor and so unlike sitting in a closed chamber, I always prefer to meet employees at their work stations irrespective of that fact whether they are white collar employees or blue collar employees. I would like to share here one incident about my meeting with a worker on one of my daily rounds. One of the operators who hailed from Uttar Pradesh shared with me his dissatisfaction towards the welfare initiatives saying that in spite of several requests he has yet not received some of the welfare items which were promised by the organization. Listening to him, I felt the need to pacify him and so as per my practice of showing warmth to an employee, I kept my hand on his shoulder and said "Bhaiya, You need to follow and meet certain criteria and then only you will receive these items. He still was not satisfied with my explanation to him and with utmost unhappiness he made an official complaint against me to the welfare committee mentioning the fact that I have disrespected him as I used the word "Bhaiya" while addressing him. Well, I missed understanding the fact that every state has a peculiar style of using words and addressing people and realized that there was a huge misunderstanding that has taken place. As the word "Bhaiya" in the state of Gujarat is addressed as "Brother", If you address someone from UP as "Bhaiya" they consider you racist. My intention of supporting the worker and helping him gain what he was eligible for turned into a major fiasco. The welfare committee presented the case to the management holding me responsible for being racist towards a worker by calling him " Bhaiya". A meeting was organized by the committee where I decided to solve the matter by apologizing to the worker and mentioned the fact that I never intended to hurt his sentiments in any manner. The situation was now in control as the worker resumed duty and so did I.

Take away for HR Buddy

While dealing with your employees, especially the blue-collar workers you should be very careful, cautious, and watchful about your behaviour towards them in any form whether it is verbal or non-verbal. Following this will avoid any kind of misunderstanding or issues that may otherwise arise. As an HR professional, you should always remember that it is very important to respect every employees' feelings, emotions, caste, creed, religion, language, eating habits, state they belong to and other related aspects to avoid hurting them in any manner and ensure a healthy working environment across the organization.

Episode 5 - Reliance Industries Ltd

My 5 years of experience in Reliance Industries has played an important role in shaping my career as an HR professional. During my tenure at Hazira, I was posted at the Polyester sector which consisted of around 800 blue collar workers and 400 white collar employees. In Blue collar workers, there was a category called TOT - trainee operator cum technician. The Job Description of the TOT was a combination of handling plant operations as well as Machine functioning. Just like in factories of various organizations, the workers in the Polyester sector at the Hazira site also had multiple grievances related to employment type, salary, benefits, canteen, and other related issues. They often showcased their dissatisfaction towards the management as all the issues were not addressed and solved as frequently as they expected. Also for the smallest of issues, they had to leave their work and walk to the HR office which added to their frustration as well as wastage of time and energy and leading to a long queue at the HR office. While I could feel the pain and discomfort of the workers, an immediate idea struck to my mind about creating a system that can bring HR department to the workers rather than the workers going to the HR department. I immediately prepared a weekly schedule of my departmental visit to the workers. I had kept a grievance register at each department and interacted with the workers from 3.00 pm in the afternoon till 6.00 pm in the evening. As the plant was working round the clock, the workers working in all the shifts could access the register, and note down their complaints if any. As per my daily practice of visiting different departments from 3.00 pm to 6.00 pm, I used to look at the register and try and resolve the complaints one by one. The mentioned practice was appreciated by all the categories of the employees and the grievance redressal process was conducted very smoothly and at a much faster pace which added to my credibility as a HR professional. I would like to share one more experience of the spinning department at the plant. In spinning departments, the functioning of Yarn machines is very crucial as the functioning of the entire plant can come to a standstill, in case of any fault with the Yarn machine. Well, workers working in this department very smartly found out ways and means of interrupting the work by quoting some or other technical issues. In spite of the maintenance engineer being available at the spot, these issues occurred very frequently. Internal friction between the workmen and the staff was also one of the reasons for this. The plant head approached me to tackle this issue and I started meeting the workers during the tea break. My regular interaction with the workers helped me understand the technicalities involved in the function of the Yarn machine. Engineer's attitude towards the work and an increased load of work was one of the reasons that emerged for non-cooperation of some of the workers. After meeting the workers and getting into the details of the problem, I started meeting shift engineer on a regular basis and along with the plant head addressed the grievances of the workers, provided the best possible solution and got the machine function properly.

Take away for HR Buddy

You should always treat your workmen like you treat your customers. The traditional system of employees approaching the HR departments should now be replaced by HR departments reaching to employees' workplaces. Interacting with employees at their respective workplaces at regular intervals will lead to enhanced employee motivation, quick addressal and resolution of the grievances and overall smooth functioning of the organization.

Episode 6 - Reliance Industries Ltd

In continuation with the above episode, I would like to share one more incident during my tenure at Hazira. There was a heavy flood in Surat and the site at Hazira was completely cut off from the city. It was announced that there would be no inward or outward traffic flow from Surat to Hazira and vice versa. So company management decided that whatever manpower was available at the site would continue doing their work so that there would be no interruption in production as there was a high stake involved in case there was disruption in the production. I was expected to play a crucial role in this situation as it was very important to ensure that the morale of the manpower remains high and the production continues without any interruption. The manpower number at the site during that time was around 1000 and it was decided that the operations will be conducted in 12 hour shifts. The crisis lasted for 4 days and the basic needs of the manpower like food, shelter and related things were completely taken care of round the clock. We also ensured to interact with the manpower on a personal level as no means of communication with the family members, could have demoralized the workers. Continuous personal interaction with the workers boosted their morale and motivated them to work. In these extraordinary circumstances, I along with my team took care of the wellbeing and the comfort of the workers and saw to it that the production is not hindered under any circumstances and as a team we succeeded in getting the desired output as per the production plan. Post the crisis, all the workers who had worked round the clock under such difficult circumstances were recognized with mementos.

Take away for HR Buddy

An elaborate planning is required in order to manage the crisis situation. It is very important to take care of the basic needs of the manpower along with continuously boosting their morale in order to ensure that the production is uninterrupted. Operating in a calm, composed and balanced manner is the prerequisite to handle the crisis situation smoothly.

Episode 7 - Bell Ceramics Ltd

I was heading the HR function at Bell Ceramics. At Bell ceramics, I embarked on my leadership journey. Bell Ceramics had two manufacturing plants. One was in the Dora town near Palej district in the state of Gujarat and the other one was at Hoskote near Bangalore in the state of Karnataka and the corporate office was based at Baroda in the state of Gujarat. One of the biggest challenges that I encountered at Dora manufacturing plant was about the blue collar workers who came from surrounding villages of Dora town. These workers were mainly engaged in farming activities and during the seasons which supported farming, these workers showcased chronic absenteeism. Their absenteeism led to shortage of skilled manpower leading to disruption in production process. So under the guidance of management, we decided to offer "Golden Handshake" and encourage chronic absentees to leave the company so that some of the activities can be outsourced leading to an uninterrupted production process. A systematic approach was adopted to achieve this objective.

In case of an absentee worker the first step was counseling which was conducted by the HR person in the presence of the union representative. The counseling session was recorded and officially signed by the worker, union representative and the HR official. After the first counseling session, if he remained absent for the second time, then again the union representative was called and the concerned worker was counseled again.

Over and above this, I and the union representative conducted home visits and tried to convince the family of the worker to ensure that the worker remains regular at the workplace. We also talked to the Sarpanch of the village that they should be grateful that the factory at their doorstep is providing them an easy opportunity of employment and thus the workers should cooperate by regularly remaining present.

These and more positive actions created a lot of pressure on the workers as well as the union. Under tremendous pressure the workers either decided to regularly remain present or continue to work at the plant or leave the company. We also decided to offer a lump sum compensation to the workers if they decide to quit the company so that they can earn livelihood in their respective villages. This technique of offering a Golden Handshake in the form of a small amount of compensation gave the desired results and a strong message reached the workers that in case they don't remain regularly present, the company will put efforts to ensure that they are on the plant regularly or else they had no other option but to leave the company with the lump sum compensation offer by the management.

With the above discussed technique, 100 workers left the company out of a total of 175. A settlement agreement was also signed with each worker to avoid any further dispute regarding this process. Golden handshake.

Take away for HR Buddy

Instead of taking a hard core legal action towards the workers, you should use alternative measures to handle issues like chronic absenteeism. Consultative measures, counseling, putting pressure on the influencers of the workers, family involvement and similar techniques need to be used to handle various kinds of indiscipline issues.

In continuation with the above episode, I would like to share one more incident during my tenure at Bell Ceramics. One day I was called by the management and was asked to get involved in devising some strategy to reduce wastage occurring at the time of different stages of the production process as this led to lesser yield and huge losses. After brainstorming with the management and other key people we came up with a strategy to monitor the wastage at each stage of the production process. With the production process divided in five stages, we decided to collect the wastage of each stage at respective places and measure the wastage for 24 hours and generate the data of wastage at each stage. During our weekly review meeting with all the section heads of each stage, we presented the compiled data which was a surprise for the section heads and there was a unanimous agreement to be committed towards the reduction of wastage. The section heads identified that the wastage occurred due to technical as well as human reasons and all of them came up with their own target of reduction of wastage. The measurement of wastage at each stage created a lot of pressure on each section head and they were committed to reduce the wastage in the best possible way. They took a lot of interest and were keen to know about the daily wastage that occurred from their respective section. In accordance with the industry standard wastage limit, we decided that the overall wastage should not exceed 5 % under any circumstances. With the continuous efforts by the whole team, the wastage was reduced to 2% which was a commendable achievement.

Take away for HR Buddy

Though as HR people we are not technically sound in production or well equipped with the knowledge about production, but with our continuous efforts and consistent endeavors we can contribution to technical departments also

Episode 9 - Bell Ceramics Ltd

Adding to one more incident at Bell Ceramics, We had an internal union and our wage settlement was due. Generally we used to sign the wage settlement for a period of 3 years but this time the management decided to sign the wage settlement for a period of 5 years. So after getting the charter of demand from the union, we organized the first meeting with the union representatives and at the beginning of the meeting we performed a Lord Ganesh Puja. During that puja, I requested the union representatives as well as the management representatives that all of us take an oath in front of Lord Ganesh about reaching to a settlement through dialogues, negotiation and deliberation, not resorting to any indiscipline in the factory premises which will hamper the production process and the decision of the Managing Director will be binding to all if the matter goes to him in case of unresolved differences. I was very much aware about the regards and respect that the workers had for the founder Managing Director and was very sure that the workers will accept whatever is his decision. Everybody agreed to take the oath on the mentioned points and within a span of 6 months the workers agreed for a wage settlement period of 5 years without the intervention of the MD.

Take away for HR Buddy

So as an HR professional, you need to understand the religious feeling of the manpower and how best you can exploit it in the interest of the company and reach a win-win situation.

One of the biggest strengths of CLP power India Ltd, where I worked for 5 years, were its power engineers with specialized knowledge and skills. They were highly intellectual and retaining these skilled power engineers was a challenge as their attrition rate was almost 15 % which is quite high as per the industry standards. In Spite of having a beautiful township, amicable culture, tremendous learning opportunities and employee friendly HR practices, retaining these engineers was very challenging.

After studying the situation, I decided to hold a meeting with the newly joined power engineers and mentor them until they settled down in the organization. So I took an initiative which was named "Coffee with Jignesh Shah". Under this initiative, I used to meet all the new employees once a month and over and above the induction programme, I used to brief them about the latest updates of the organization that included policies and processes, growth, value system, achievements, major milestones and related processes. Through this monthly meeting they also had a platform to share their personal as well as professional issues. It was made very clear that general/common issues will be discussed in a common forum and resolved amicably as soon as possible and personal issues were addressed on one to one basis in a private forum. Every month I used to meet these engineers at the mentioned forum. When the engineers spent a tenure of six months in the organization, they would leave the forum and the new recruits would join. Nevertheless those who left the forum were always welcomed in case they wanted to meet for any discussion. The engineers were very happy about the initiative of monthly meetings. The initiative increased their engagement towards the work as well as the organization, increased their motivation and opened up a lot of learning and development opportunities for them which reduced the attrition rate from 15 % to 10 %.

Take away for HR Buddy

It is very important for HR professionals to meet their employees and have one to one or general meetings at regular intervals. HR professionals must provide a forum to their employees to vent out their feelings, emotions and grievances which will then be addressed followed by a solution. This will enhance the commitment and loyalty of the employees and add to the retention ratio.

Episode 11- CLP Power India Ltd

In continuation with the above episode, I would like to share one more experience during my tenure at CLP Power India Ltd about engaging the young power engineers. I introduced a theme based managerial talent hunt competition. So on a given theme, a cross functional team consisted of 3 members. As the word cross functional team says itself that the team consisted of employees from different departments. The teams were asked to make presentations on the allotted theme and the time allotted for the presentation was 15 minutes which included 5 minutes of Questions and Answers. The competition was evaluated by an external panel of judges which too was cross functional. The panel was a combination of leaders from industry, academia and NGO. The initiative was hugely supported and participated by the employees. Nearly 40 % engineers participated in this competition. The competition helped them to hone their presentation skills as well as communication skills. They learned the art of expression of thoughts and could add on their behavioral as well as soft skills. The power engineers participated wholeheartedly in this initiative and considered this to be a great learning experience for them towards their journey of becoming effective and efficient managers as well as leaders.

Take away for HR Buddy

It is very important for HR professionals to think out of the box and implement innovative initiatives. These initiatives should be aimed at enhancing the skill of the manpower and making the jobs more interesting.

Episode 12 - JMC Projects (I) Ltd

In 2010, I joined JMC projects (I) Ltd, an infrastructure company with a large number of projects and manpower. An industry of different type as the employees were to work under hard circumstances against nature and follow tight deadlines. There were 75 operational projects with around 10,000 employees. Attrition and retaining quality manpower was a big challenge at JMC. On analyzing the attrition data it was found that around 25 % to 30 % of the new joinees left the company within six months of their joining and another 20 % to 25 % new joinees left the organization within one year of their joining. We could see that the employees were not settling down at their respective sites and in their initial stage of their association they were not taken care of properly in respect of the basic hygiene factors. In order to tackle this problem, I took the initiative of conducting stay interviews. A questionnaire was designed for the same which was used while conducting a stay interview. The stay interview was designed with an aim to conduct the interview of a newly joined employee at different stages. Due to sites located at multiple locations, it was decided the HR team from the head office will be conducting telephonic stay interviews of the new joinees. The stay interview was conducted at three stages. The first stage was conducting the interview in the first month of joining, then conducting the interview after three months of joining and then at the end of six months of joining. During the first month of joining we inquired about the availability of the basic needs like food, shelter, sanitation to the employees. It was also checked whether they were provided support with respect to site induction, clarity on reporting relationships, and technical well as infrastructural resources. After three months of joining we inquired whether the employee had been properly engaged in the assigned task, whether they got proper support from their seniors at the site, whether they got sufficient needed resources in order to perform the duty. After 6 months on the completion of the probation period, we inquired how well the employees had settled in these six months,whether they were enjoying their respective jobs, what were their future plans, whether they were getting enough opportunities to showcase their skills, abilities, knowledge and expertise.

This helped the HR professional know about the lapses in the system and understand the reasons for attrition. Some of the employees had issues on the above mentioned facilities at different stages and thus the HR department decided to work on the lapses and take all the necessary corrective action to provide all the committed services to the employees. It was ensured that all the new joinees got all the support, facilities as well as services that were committed to them at the time of joining the organization which will help them in settling down at their new working environment. With this approach we made sure that at the end of six months new joinees are settled in the organization and they look forward to a long and healthy association with the company. This initiative was highly appreciated by the employees as well as the management and helped the company reduce attrition rate of the new joinees drastically.

Take away for HR Buddy

New joinees in the beginning always look forward for a mentor or a buddy and thus it is very important for HR professionals to regularly remain in touch with the new joinees. This will help the HR professionals to understand the way they are settling and address the issues or challenges they are facing in the initial tenure at the organization. Quick address and resolution of the issues will enhance the retention ratio of the new joinees.

Episode 13 - Montecarlo Ltd

At Montecarlo Ltd I had realized the fact that it was very important for MCL to move away from offering training to building a training culture which was unheard of in many companies in their industry and thus In this episode I would like to share my experience of creating HR Automation and building a culture of training while streamlining the entire L & D function. MCL introduced SAP platform in the company way back in 2008. It was one of the first major construction companies to embark on the path of becoming automated and integrating and aligning all its processes through digital platforms. This was indeed a huge challenge and was not a routine thing in the heavy industry especially in the construction industry. But MCL was committed to provide superior experience and effective services to its employees as well as customers and so pushed through to implement SAP and HR Automation throughout the company and I played an instrumental role in the process of HR automation. Some of the HR processes that were automated included Human Resource Planning, Recruitment and Selection, Induction, Training, Compensation and Performance Management which otherwise was a rare thing for a construction company to adopt. All the systems were very user friendly and could be accessed through one's mobile phones as well. Also, this automation facilitated business and people decision making in real time with ease, speed and efficiency. A robust HR automation infrastructure was also ensured across company's verticals and domains. All the processes were integrated and aligned to work digitally. The fear of the unknown invited some resistance, but the merits of HR automation far exceeded its apprehensions and led to a successful implementation of HR Automation.

Now talking about building a culture of training while streamlining the entire L&D function at Montecarlo. With the changes in the company that HR automation brought, I also felt that this was the right time to integrate the paths of L&D and HR and also adopt automation in the HR processes, especially the Learning and Development function. Training in construction industries is mostly technical and in general; needs to be driven, mandatory, or routine. People participate in training more to upgrade their knowledge or technical skills or get new information around their processes, areas of expertise, work domain, or machinery they deal with. While this could have remained the same for MCL as well, I had a bigger and broader vision. I wanted to build a culture of training at Montecarlo. My vision of training was to build a new perspective towards training and let people participate fully and wholeheartedly in training as a tool for self-discovery, skill enhancement and repertoire building. One of my bigger challenges was to automate the training function right from training need identification, training development, training delivery up to training evaluation. With constant support and motivation from the Joint Managing Directors; I initiated my efforts of not only building a training infrastructure but of building a positive and healthy mind-set towards training among people at MCL. I took the first step towards this by developing SOPs for all the departments. The same was done through project UDAAN with the help of KPMG. These SOPs became a light post for all design and development of training at MCL. We created 46 pre-identified competencies and 10 types of behavioral training based on the identified competencies and effective mapping of these competencies. The training was divided into four broad categories which were Induction Program (for all new joinees),Mandatory Training (to understand the SOPs), Functional Training (based on competency mapping),Behavioral Training (based on behavioral competencies). It was decided that all the training except behavioural training will be conducted by in house trainers. As mentioned above, the 46 competencies were created for 142 roles in the company. A quarterly training calendar was prepared and training needs were identified on the basis of the identified competencies which was then followed by allotting employees to various training. All the phases of training which included training need identification, training delivery, training implementation and training evaluation were conducted very smoothly. I knew that what me and joint MDs had initiated and created is just the beginning of what can be an exemplary industry practice tomorrow. But it needed sustained efforts and continuous push for the employees to start believing in the philosophy of learning and developing. I was also sure that the training culture at Montecarlo will come full circle when people take ownership of their own development and work hard towards achieving it. This indeed will also take Montecarlo to greater heights of organizational excellence and people empowerment.

Take away for HR Buddy

In today's competitive world the HR function needs to be upgraded with every passing day inorder to remain in pace with the external environment especially the competitors. Irrespective of the industry, HR automation can be implemented smoothly if planned properly.

2.2 *Unique HR Initiatives*

ATM- All Time Mitra

Challenge: Adjustment of a new employee to a new environment, culture, people, role, etc.

Process: As much as employers are looking for new employees to make a good first impression during their first few days in a new job, the same way employees are looking to their employers to also make such kind of impression. New hires begin their first day with excitement and enthusiasm, but this spirit can be enhanced or destroyed, depending on the employee's first impression of the organization. What happens during the first few days will determine the employee's perception of the company and the staff they are working with. As an HRBP, to embrace this challenge and in order to handhold in light of organization dynamics and complexities with a clear objective that new talent will settle down well in the organization, especially if the organization has a long legacy, the "All Time Mitra- ATM" initiative will help build a personal connection with a co-worker, the organization and may accelerate the productivity of new hires and enhance job satisfaction, so that the new employees stay with the company. HRBP needs to facilitate and help the new talent to understand the working protocol and working etiquette of the organization. New Talent is also expected to know the key stakeholders, key people, and colleagues, along with their background, and working style. Once the new entrant is clear, it will be easy and comfortable for them to adjust to the business culture. As an HRBP, we need to play the role of an ATM. We must gain the trust of the new employees so that they feel comfortable in approaching us for any issue related to systems processes or culture. Once the employee settles down easily, it becomes easier for the new employee to start performing and contributing at the earliest. Satisfaction at a professional and personal level increases due to the same. In order to gain the trust of new employees ATM must possess the following qualities:

◆ Helping attitude

◆ Transparent Communication

◆ System and process orientation mind-set

ATM is not just beneficiary to the new employee, it's a good way to develop some job enrichment and skills of existing staff members. The 'Mitra' will learn more about the business, and its employees as well as gain valuable mentoring and leadership skills that'll be useful within the company.

Outcome: Problem-solving with transparency and friendly approach

Stay Interview

Challenge: Exposure of a new employee to a new culture, people, and role

Process: Another useful initiative is the stay interview. Many employees may not be familiar with the concept of Stay Interviews. They might have a perception that it's the management's way to negotiate and impose strategies. Therefore as an HRBP, it's important to start by explaining why you're conducting the interview and what type of information you'll be discussing. Here our goal is to gain insight into what motivates and frustrates our employees, what they value in the organization, and how to support, develop, and retain them. Also to build and strengthen your relationship, and ultimately discover the key to keeping their engagement levels high. To conduct an effective stay interview standard structured questions in an informal conversational manner helps in finding out whether the new employee has settled well or not. One can also check whether the working relationship is clear or not. If any employee has multiple reports then it should be made clear, what to report to whom as per feedback. We as HRBP must initiate necessary communication and ensure their comfort level is maintained. This initiative helps in increasing the level of trust and credibility as an HRBP. It helps in gaining specific information and create individualized strategies that cater to stop or offset reasons why employees would leave. Here, the purpose of the Stay Interview is to gain useful information, show appreciation, and remind employees that they are important to the organization. The employee feels they are important just by the fact that the organization is concerned about their future and that their manager took the time to consult with them

Outcome: Realization of importance, each resource at work is important!

Coffee with VP-HR/ Head-HR

Challenge: Employees often have issues but they do not know who to approach or what to do

Process: In many organizations reaching out to the senior leadership family is only for the Managers and above category of people where Executives and shop floor workers can only do that through channels of middle management. As an HRBP to rectify and foster change in the communication channel within the organization this initiative of "Coffee with VP " is prescribed. The spirit of "Coffee with VP " initiative is to foster and promote the culture of openness and transparent communication, where we plan to gather our employees, to have informal conversations with our Vice President. This will have our employees interact directly with the VP and they can openly share any ideas, suggestions, grievances, or informal discussions. Resulting in increased connection and range of better ideas and suggestions to emerge. This is a good informal way to create communication channels and promote transparency in the workplace.

Outcome: Reduce various grievances among employees with a fair approach to the HR team!

Managerial Talent Hunt

Challenge: Lack of platform to improve presentation and public speaking skills

Process: It is not only necessary to keep a new employee hooked but it is equally important to ensure that the existing ones are also well attended. Every individual in an organization has their individual goals which usually get hindered in achieving the organizational goals. To cater to this challenge employees need a platform to nurture and present their skills. For this another unique employee engagement initiative is to keep the zeal and enthusiasm of the employees upbeat is Management Talent Hunt. It is one such event wherein to develop managerial skills among our employees, this initiative was launched. Employees form cross functional team of 3 members and prepare a presentation on a given topic. Each team is given 15-20 minutes to make the presentation. Each team even after having the same topic have a varied perspective towards the same. The presentation is then followed by a Question & Answer session by the esteemed panel of external judges, who evaluate the presentation based on the contents matching the theme of the topic, presentation style and confidence level to handle the questions from the judges. The 3 winning teams are rewarded and provided certificates of appreciation, all the participants are also given a certificate of participation to encourage them for such future endeavors. This initiative brings forward many employees willing to showcase their ideas and skills and also helps management identify hidden stars among the lot.

Outcome: Boost the vocational and presentation skills of Managers to make them presentable and confident speakers

The Knowledge Cafe

Challenge: There are many individual knowledge-sharing barriers that people from the working class face these days, like a general lack of time to Share knowledge, and time to identify colleagues in need of specific knowledge

Process: Another such initiative is the knowledge sharing forum "The Knowledge Cafe". The agenda of this is to bring together our employees to learn newer concepts and discuss various topics to gain knowledge by sharing with each other. This voluntary forum's topic range is limitless and healthy discussions for mutual benefits are welcome. Any interested employee gets an opportunity to share his/her knowledge on the topic which he has gained through reading books and or any other sources. Such a gathering can be planned on the 3rd Monday of every month after work hours to make sure that our routine work does not get affected. For the benefit of other employees who could not make it to the meeting one can share an executive summary of the same on the next day which briefly sums up the meeting; it includes major points that were discussed during the meeting and also the key learnings gained out of the same. Helps in providing a platform to freely share and discuss new happenings, events or information

Outcome: Knowledge Sharing & breaking the ice at work place among colleagues

Challenge: Employees have a lot of different problems, and different challenges to face in their normal life. What seems a problem for one person might be a luxury for another. Hence, people have very different ideas to face stress in their normal life.

Process: To cater to this challenge, Employee Counselling is initiated. So not just knowledge sharing, if any employee wishes to share something private and wants to keep their confidentiality intact, we have an initiative for that as well; wherein an employee can share his /her personal problem/grievance with us. It not only helps in reducing the stress level of the employee but also tries and provide the best possible solutions. Employee counseling gives individuals a valuable opportunity to work through problems and stresses in a strictly confidential and supportive atmosphere. Counseling provides access to several basic forms of helping: giving information, direct action, teaching and coaching, advocacy, and providing feedback and advice, for example, counseling involves the individual employee meeting which is on a one-on-one basis. This encourages discussion of personal and work-related difficulties. This is often followed by the adoption of an active problem-solving approach to tackle the problems at hand. As an organization, we always strive to bring newer, better, and unique ways to ensure our employees are not just well engaged but also looked after as in a tight-knit family.

Outcome: Generating a problem-solving approach to tackle difficult situations at the workplace which gives an enormous confidence boost to employees!

*****

3 : The path to wisdom

3.1 Ten Pearls of wisdom

With my passion towards the HR profession and multifaceted working experience, I have got enormous opportunities to deal with a multigenerational workforce. I take great pride in sharing that I have groomed a lot of young professionals who are today holding a respectable position in the HR domain. In today's highly competitive and ever changing business world it is very important to groom the younger generation so that they are well equipped with the right knowledge and skills to excel in their jobs.

During my journey of more than three decades of seeing people reach great heights, settling in challenging roles, facing career stagnation and failing miserably, I have gathered some valuable learning, which I call - "Ten Pearls of Wisdom".

Let me take you through these Ten valuable pearls

1. Focus

Focus plays a very crucial role in the success saga of any person. Indian mythology has numerous narrations about victories obtained by focus. The famous story of Arjuna about shooting an arrow in the eye of the bird is a classic example of one's focus toward the achievement of a goal. While working in an environment with numerous distractions, one has to work towards the development of ability to focus. With the advent of social media and up gradation of technology every minute, it has now become inevitable to learn to focus on the goals and strive towards achieving them. Prioritizing is a key skill towards working efficiently as well as effectively. A person should be able to focus both on personal as well as professional goals. Focus proves to be an effective tool if used at all the phases of life and at every juncture of one's career. It has to be developed and applied in a wholesome manner. For Eg: A college going student divides his/her goal in a short term and long term pattern. His short team goal should be to focus on lectures and understand the classroom training inorder to attain the long term goal of attaining placement in a reputed organization or start or join his/her own business. So the long term focus is attaining a job or starting a business and short term focus is to attend the lectures with utmost sincerity. While at home a person should focus on spending quality time with one's family and invest time on one's self as well. Balance between personal and professional life is a key towards a happy life both as a person as well as a professional. Quoting an example of my association with a young professional during my tenure with a MNC, I always appreciated his knowledge, skills and intelligence. However, he lacked the ability to focus and concentrate on his work and often used to make personal calls during office hours and then work during late hours at the office inorder to complete his pending work. I mentored as well as coached him to develop his ability to focus and made him realize the importance of the same if he wanted to develop a successful career. An ability to focus will lead to high quality performance, timely completion of the work and successful achievement of goals.

2. Critical Observation

Critical observation is beyond criticizing someone. It is basically developing a critical view point about an object, situation, event or a person. It is a way to recognize problems before others do and is a way to handle problems and related situations tactfully. It involves asking questions to oneself as to why am I doing this? How significant is the work that I am doing? Am I performing as expected by my superiors? Is my work going to add any value to my department as well as the organization? Am I going to learn something while doing this work? All these answers are very necessary to work effectively. Performing a task just for the sake of it is not going to give you as well as the organization the desired results. However, if you ask the above mentioned questions to yourself before you start working on a particular assignment, it is definitely going to enhance the quality of the work and job satisfaction. Asking yourself What, When, Why, Where and How will add to your sense of fulfillment and you will enjoy doing your job.

3. Common sense

People often fail to understand the importance and elegance of common sense. Quoting an old saying "Common sense is not very common", I would like to share a fact that most of the people do not apply this not because of their inability to apply it but because of their relaxed, casual or ignorant attitude. I have come across many professionals in my career who do not want to think about a task from multiple angles. They often do not make any efforts to break the task into multiple components to derive a logical solution. A complicated task becomes extremely simple if one applies common sense to it. I have seen people failing miserably in their pursuit towards achievement of their goals just by the reason of not applying common sense. These people generally belong to a lot who resist change in all forms and under every circumstance. They do not remain updated about the latest developments nor do they apply their learning from earlier tasks or previous organizations. They are happy and satisfied in their mundane working style. Applying common sense is very crucial whether it is your personal life or professional life. I would just like to say that common sense is about seeing solutions in the problem rather than seeing problems in the solution.

4. Passion for work

Success without passion becomes a farsighted dream. One need to be passionate about the profession which he/she belongs to. It is an inner drive that inspires as well as motivates a person to work hard, learn more, face challenges, overcome hurdles, dream big and pursue relentlessly towards the achievement of goals. A passionate person always looks for excellence in any task allotted to him/her. Passion has led people to build successful professional careers. Mother Teresa, the greatest humanitarian of the 20th century, devoted her entire life to helping poor and needy people as she was extremely passionate about community service. The passion for innovation that Steve Jobs possessed has changed the way people are looking at technology. He often quoted that "The only way to do great work is to love what you do. If you have not found it yet, keep looking, don't settle". All the people who have been legends in their own fields, whether it is sports, cinema, politics, medicine, law, teaching, various facets of the corporate world and many more sung as well as unsung professionals have always been known as legends as they have had enormous passion for their work. While getting disappointed, demotivated as well as frustrated while performing a task, just thinking about your name attached to that task will keep your spirits high and convert your apprehensions to encouragement, thereby paving way towards successful completion of the task assigned.

5. Self- discipline

Self - discipline is more of a habit rather than ability or skill. Immense research on self-discipline says that people with self-discipline are clear about the choices that they wish to make; actions they need to take and can easily manage conflicting situations. They are more on a rational side rather than being emotional. They do not let emotions, imaginations and assumptions handle their decisions. The list of habits that fall under self-discipline is a long one but some of those are being punctual, eating healthy, eating at the right time, daily exercise, daily reading, waking up early. There was a young and bright girl in one of the organizations where I worked. A professional who was extremely immaculate in her work, very high on conceptual clarity, communication and customer relationships. Her seniors would always appreciate her approach towards work and would always consider her in case of any tough assignments or situations. But she lacked one of the most important aspects of self-discipline which was punctuality. She often used to come late to the office, late to the meetings with the customers as well as senior management and she paid a huge price for this behaviour by losing her job. Self-discipline is inevitable to achieve success. It has to be present in your thoughts, behaviour as well as actions.

6. Empathy

Empathy is the ability to understand the problems or feelings of the other person, seeing things from their view point and imagining you at their place. When a person is empathetic to the emotions of a particular person, that person develops a sense of comfort which leads to development of a bond and establishment of rapport. In the professional world it is very important to build strong rapport with your associates as networking is the key to a successful professional relationship. A person always confides in an empathetic person and develops a relationship of trust and faith. So along with sympathy, empathy is equally important to develop a successful professional career

7. Timely communication

Communication is the key to the door of success. It is an art to exchange one's thoughts and ideas in a manner that can be easily understood by the other person. But timeliness and communication are like two sides of the same coin. Communication as a skill is only important when it is done at the right time. Communication that is not done at the right time loses its meaning and value. Timely communication will help the person in both personal as well as professional life and it will prove to be a great support to the organizations in getting the best out of every opportunity through informed decision making. Once during my association with one of the organizations, I had lined up an interview with a person who was supposed to travel for the same from a distant place which was required that person to travel for two days in order to make it to the interview meeting. Due to a business exigency I had to cancel this interview meeting and I had told one of my team members' to communicate the same to the concerned. Due to negligent attitude, the team member missed timely communication and informed the same to the concerned when he had already begun the journey. The concerned person faced a lot of difficulties as he had to get down in the middle of the journey, stay in a hotel and could reach back to his home the next day. This not only led to disturbed the schedule of the person but also created an unprofessional image of the HR department as well as the organization in multiple contexts. Hence one must understand that effective, smooth and timely communication definitely leads to seamless and successful execution of the tasks undertaken.

8. Quick Response

In today's fast and dynamic world, quick response is very imperative. It is one of the key factors that lead to enhanced credibility of a HR professional. A skill that is the easiest to adopt but most of the people fail in doing so. While educating you all with this pearl of wisdom, let me clarify that a quick response without studying the situation will backfire and hence one should understand and analyze the situation before responding. A logical quick response is only possible if it is backed by clarity of thoughts and understanding strengths, weaknesses, opportunities and threats of the problem or situation. Responding quickly can also be considered as a component of self-discipline. One must understand the importance of prioritization and should ensure that no matter remains pending. Quick response has taken people to great heights and changed their lives for the better. It also makes the other person feel important and passes a strong message that you are considering his/her time equally important as yours. Quick response adds to the reputation and goodwill of the person as well as the organization.

9. Networking

In today's scenario in order to get our work done and to be more competitive, networking with the right kind of professionals is very important. Networking helps a person to become more resourceful and face today's challenging times in a dynamic way and exploit the business opportunities in a much more effective way. It is a way of developing connections that can provide you with contacts and advices that can further help you in making informed career decisions. One of the easiest and the upgraded ways of getting connected to a large number of professionals is Linked in, Facebook, Instagram, Twitter and other related social media platforms. So sharing my personal example, let me talk about my networking on social media platforms like Linked In, Facebook, Instagram and Twitter. I have been using Linked In extensively to facilitate myself in professional work. It has helped me connect with professionals as well a leaders across the globe. The network that I have developed here has helped me spot multiple talents and enhance my professional career in multiple ways. Networking is the need of the hour and as it is rightly said "Network is Networth"

10. Techsavvy

It is very important for professionals to have good knowledge and understanding of modern technology. One should possess the right skills and knowledge to operate the modern devices effectively. Being IT Savvy is the prerequisite in today's scenario, irrespective of one's designation, work experience, age or qualification. One must ensure that he/she is aware about the basics of computers that includes MS Office and email management. It is also very important to handle social media independently and express yourself electronically without anyone's support. Quoting myself, I was not very proficient as far as the use of computers was concerned. But I was very sure that I need to learn the same at the earliest to remain in pace with the fast moving world. So I decided to attend a three month evening computer course and learnt the whole module of M S office. This helped me enhance my working capacity and need not depend on any of my teammates. The best example of the advantage of being IT Savvy is using technology during the time of Corona Pandemic. It helped everyone connect with their colleagues as well as relatives. Being IT savvy, helped all the people to take care of their personal as well as professional life. Hence I strongly believe that one must constantly remain upgraded with the latest technologies to remain relevant in their professions.

My years of experience have enabled me to conceive these pearls which in practice have helped me achieve success in all facets of life. I am confident that for those who will chant these pearls, practice the same, introspect and take corrective action on a daily basis, success in every walk of life is inevitable for them. Chanting these pearls on a daily basis will always reinforce your mind-set and motivate you to practice them in your daily life.

3.2   Chhoti Chhoti Baatein

1. Master Piece

A little boy went to his old grandpa and asked, "What's the value of life?" The grandpa gave him one stone and said, "Find out the value of this stone, but don't sell it." The boy took the stone to an Orange Seller and asked him what its cost would be. The Orange Seller saw the shiny stone and said, "You can take 12 oranges and give me the stone." The boy apologized and said that the grandpa has asked him not to sell it. He went ahead and found a vegetable seller. "What could be the value of this stone?" he asked the vegetable seller. The seller saw the shiny stone and said, "Take one sack of potatoes and give me the stone. The boy again apologized and said he can't sell it. Further ahead, he went into a jewellery shop and asked the value of the stone. The jeweler saw the stone under a lens and said, "I'll give you 1 million for this stone." When the boy shook his head, the jeweler said, "Alright, alright, take 2 24karat gold necklaces, but give me the stone." The boy explained that he can't sell the stone. Further ahead, the boy saw a precious stone's shop and asked the seller the value of this stone. When the precious stone's seller saw the big ruby, he lay down a red cloth and put the ruby on it. Then he walked in circles around the ruby and bent down and touched his head in front of the ruby. '`From where did you bring this priceless ruby from?" he asked. "Even if I sell the whole world, and my life, I won't be able to purchase this priceless stone." Stunned and confused, the boy returned to the grandpa and told him what had happened. "Now tell me what is the value of life, grandpa?" Grandpa said, "The answers you got from the Orange Seller, the Vegetable Seller, the Jeweler & the Precious Stone's Seller explain the value of our life... You may be a precious stone, even priceless, but, people will value you based on their financial status, their level of information, their belief in you, and their motive behind entertaining you, their ambition, and their risk-taking ability. But don't fear, you will surely find someone who will discern your true value." Respect yourself, don't sell yourself cheap, you are rare, Unique, Original, and the only one of our kind, you are a masterpiece because you are MASTER'S PIECE, No one can Replace you. Value the value...

Life Lessons: Every individual is unique and gifted. So value yourself.

2. 1000 Mirror

A person asked a question to his Guru, "My workers are not true to me. My children, my wife, and the entire world are very selfish. Nobody is correct."Guru smiled and told a story. In one small village there was a room with 1000 mirrors. One small girl used to go inside and play. Seeing thousands of children around her she was joyful. She would clap her hands and all the 1000 children would clap back at her. She considered this place as the world's happiest and beautiful place and would visit it often. This same place was once visited by a sad and a depressed person. He saw around him thousands of angry men staring at him. He got scared and raised his hands to hit them and in return 1000 hands lifted to hit him back. He thought... This is the worst place in the world and left that place. This world is also a room with 1000 mirrors around you... What we let out of us is what society will give back to us.

Life Lessons: This world is a heaven... It's up to us what we make out of it...

3. Love

A woman saw 3 saints in front of her house. She did not know any of them. She said – "Kindly come inside and have food." The saints replied – "Is your husband inside the house?" Woman – "No, he has gone out." Saints – "Will step into the house only when he is there." In the evening when the woman's husband returns home, she tells him about the saints. Husband – "Go and tell them I am home, and invite them inside the house." She went out and called the saints inside the house. The saints now said – "We all don't go inside anyone's house together." "But why?" – The woman asked. One of the saints replied – "My name is wealth." Then he pointed to the other saints and said – "These two saints' names are 'prosperity' and 'love'. Only one of us can come inside your house! You go in, discuss with your family, and decide which saint you want to invite." The woman went inside and told her husband all about this. He was excited. He said – "If this is the matter, let us invite wealth! Our house will then be filled with happiness." Wife – "I feel we should invite prosperity."Their daughter was in the next room. She was listening to the discussions. She came outside and said – "I feel we should invite love. Nothing is more important." "You are right, we should invite love only." – Her parents agreed. The woman went out and asked the saints – "Who is love? Please come inside the house." Love started walking towards the house! The other two saints started following love. The surprised woman asked the saints – "I only invited love. Why are you two also coming inside the house?" One of the saints replied – "If you had invited prosperity or wealth, only that saint would have entered your house. But you have invited love! Love never walks alone. Wherever there's love, there's prosperity and wealth. They all go hand in hand." Read this story once, twice, thrice... If you like it, stay with love.

Life Lessons: Spread love, give love and take love. As love is the only secret to success!!!

4. Red Rose and the Cactus'

One beautiful spring day a red rose blossomed in a forest. Many kinds of trees and plants grew there. As the rose looked around, a pine tree nearby said, "What a beautiful flower. I wish I was that lovely." Another tree said, "Dear pine, do not be sad, we cannot have everything." The rose turned its head and remarked, "It seems that I am the most beautiful plant in this forest." A sunflower raised its yellow head and asked, "Why do you say that? In this forest there are many beautiful plants. You are just one of them." The red rose replied, "I see everyone looking at me and admiring me." Then the rose looked at a cactus and said, "Look at that ugly plant full of thorns!" The pine tree said, "Red rose, what kind of talk is this? Who can say what beauty is? You have thorns too." The proud red rose looked angrily at the pine and said, "I thought you had good taste! You do not know what beauty is at all. You cannot compare my thorns to that of the cactus." "What a proud flower", thought the trees. The rose tried to move its roots away from the cactus, but it could not move. As the days passed, the red rose would look at the cactus and say insulting things, like: This plant is useless? How sorry I am to be his neighbor." The cactus never got upset and he even tried to advise the rose, saying, "God did not create any form of life without a purpose." Spring passed, and the weather became very warm. Life became difficult in the forest, as the plants and animals needed water and no rain fell. The red rose began to wilt. One day the rose saw sparrows stick their beaks into the cactus and then fly away, refreshed. This was puzzling, and the red rose asked the pine tree what the birds were doing. The pine tree explained that the birds got water from the cactus. "Does it not hurt when they make holes?" asked the rose. "Yes, but the cactus does not like to see any birds suffer," replied the pine. The rose opened its eyes in wonder and said, "The cactus has water?" "Yes, you can also drink from it. The sparrow can bring water to you if you ask the cactus for help." The red rose felt too ashamed of its past words and behavior to ask for water from the cactus, but then it finally did ask the cactus for help. The cactus kindly agreed and the birds filled their beaks with water and watered the rose's roots.

Life Lessons: The rose and all of us learned a lesson never judge anyone by their appearance again. God did not create anything without a purpose.

5. Be an Eagle and not a Duck

I was waiting in line for a ride at the airport in Dubai. When a cab pulled up, the first thing I noticed was that the taxi was polished to a bright shine. Smartly dressed in white shirt, black tie, and freshly pressed black slacks, the cab driver jumped out and rounded the car to open the back passenger door for me. He handed me a laminated card and said: 'I'm Abdul, your driver. While I'm loading your bags in the trunk I'd like you to read my mission statement.' Taken aback, I read the card. It said: Abdul's Mission Statement: To get my customers to their destination in the quickest, safest, and cheapest way possible in a friendly environment. This blew me away. Especially when I noticed that the inside of the cab matched the outside. Spotlessly clean! As he slid behind the wheel, Abdul said, 'Would you like a cup of coffee? I have a thermos of regular and one of decaf.'I said jokingly, 'No, I'd prefer a soft drink.' Abdul smiled and said, 'No problem. I have a cooler up front with regular and Diet Coke, lassi, water, and orange juice.' Almost stuttering, I said, 'I'll take a Lassi. 'Handing me my drink, Abdul said,

'If you'd like something to read, I have The NST, Star, and Sun Today.' As they were pulling away, Abdul handed me another laminated card, 'These are the stations I get and the music they play if you'd like to listen to the radio.' As if that weren't enough, Abdul told me that he had the air conditioning on and asked if the temperature was comfortable for me. Then he advised me of the best route to my destination for that time of day. He also let me know that he'd be happy to chat and tell me about some of the sights or, if I preferred, to leave me with my own thoughts. 'Tell me, Abdul,' I was amazed and asked him, 'Have you always served customers like this?' Abdul smiled into the rearview mirror. "No, not always. In fact, it's only been in the last two years. My first five years driving, I spent most of my time complaining like all the rest of the cabbies do. Then I heard about POWER OF CHOICE one day." Power of choice is that you can be a duck or an eagle. 'If you get up in the morning expecting to have a bad day, you'll rarely disappoint yourself. Stop complaining!' 'Don't be a duck. Be an eagle. Ducks quack and complain. Eagles soar above the crowd.' 'That hit me. Really hard' said Abdul. 'It is about me. I was always quacking and complaining, so I decided to change my attitude and become an eagle. I looked around at the other cabs and their drivers. The cabs were dirty, the drivers were unfriendly, and the customers were unhappy. So I decided to make some changes, slowly... a few at a time. When my customers responded well, I did more.' 'I take it that it has paid off for you,' I said. 'It sure has,' Abdul replied. 'My first year as an eagle, I doubled my income from the previous year. This year I'll probably quadruple it. My customers call me for appointments on my cell phone or leave a message on it.' Abdul made a different choice. He decided to stop quacking like a duck and start soaring like an eagle. Start becoming an eagle today... one small step every week. Next week... And next...And.... A great Thought... "You don't die if you fall in the water, you die only if you don't swim." That's the Real Meaning of Life.

Life Lessons: Improve yourself and your skills in a different way. Be an eagle. Not a Duck.

6. The 99 Club

Once upon a time, there lived a King who, despite his luxurious lifestyle, was neither happy nor content. One day, the King came upon a servant who was singing happily while he worked. This fascinated the King; why was he, the Supreme Ruler of the Land, unhappy and gloomy, while a lowly servant had so much joy in his heart? The King asked the servant, "Why are you so happy?" The man replied, "Your Majesty, I am nothing but a servant, but my family and I don't need too much - just a roof over our heads and warm food to fill our tummies." Later in the day, the King sought the advice of his most trusted advisor. After hearing the King's woes and the servant's story, the advisor said," Your Majesty, I believe that the servant has not been made part of The 99 Club." "The 99 Club? And what exactly is that?" the King inquired. The advisor replied, "Your Majesty, to truly know what The 99 Club is, place 99 Gold coins in a bag and leave it at this servant's doorstep." When the servant saw the bag, he took it into his house. When he opened the bag, he let out a great shout of joy... so many gold coins! He began to count them. After several counts, he was at last convinced that there were 99 coins. He wondered, "What could've happened to that last gold coin? Surely, no one would leave 99 coins!" He looked everywhere he could, but that final coin was elusive. Finally, exhausted, he decided that he was going to have to work harder than ever to earn that gold coin and complete his collection. From that day, the servant's life was changed. He was overworked, horribly grumpy, and castigated his family for not helping him make that 100th gold coin. He stopped singing while he worked. Witnessing this drastic transformation, the King was puzzled. When he sought his advisor's help, the advisor said, "Your Majesty, the servant has now officially joined The 99 Club."He continued, "The 99 Club is a name given to those people who have enough to be happy but are never contented because they're always yearning and striving for that extra 1 to round it out to 100! We can be happy, even with very little in our lives, but the minute we're given something bigger and better, we want even more! We lose our sleep, and our happiness, we hurt the people around us; all these as a price for our growing needs and desires. That's what joining The 99 Club is all about."

Life Lessons: Be Happy with what you have.

7. Discover the 90/10 Principle

It will change your life (at least the way you react to situations). What is this principle? 10% of life is made up of what happens to you. 90% of life is decided by how you react. What does this mean? We really have no control over 10% of what happens to us. We cannot stop the car from breaking down. The plane will be late arriving, which throws our whole schedule off. A driver may cut us off in traffic. We have no control over this 10%. The other 90% is different. You determine the other 90%. How? ....By your reaction. You cannot control a red light. but you can control your reaction. Don't let people fool you; YOU can control how you react. Let's use an example. You are eating breakfast with your family. Your daughter knocks over a cup of coffee onto your business shirt. You have no control over what just happened. What happens next will be determined by how you react. You curse. You harshly scold your daughter for knocking the cup over. She breaks down in tears. After scolding her, you turn to your spouse and criticize her for placing the cup too close to the edge of the table. A short verbal battle follows. You storm upstairs and change your shirt. Back downstairs, you find your daughter has been too busy crying to finish breakfast and get ready for school. She misses the bus. Your spouse must leave immediately for work. You rush to the car and drive your daughter to school. Because you are late, you drive 40 miles an hour in a 30 mph speed limit. After a 15-minute delay and throwing a $60 traffic fine away, you arrive at school. Your daughter runs into the building without saying goodbye. After arriving at the office 20 minutes late, you find you forgot your briefcase. Your day has started terribly. As it continues, it seems to get worse and worse. You look forward to coming home. When you arrive home, you find a small wedge in your relationship with your spouse and daughter. Why? .... Because of how you reacted in the morning. Why did you have a bad day? A) Did the coffee cause it? B) Did your daughter cause it? C) Did the policeman cause it? D) Did you cause it? The answer is "D". You had no control over what happened with the coffee. How you reacted in those 5 seconds is what caused your bad day. Here is what could have and should have happened. Coffee splashes over you. Your daughter is about to cry. You gently say, "Its ok honey, you just need to be more careful next time". Grabbing a towel you rush upstairs. After grabbing a new shirt and your briefcase, you come back down in time to look through the window and see your child getting on the bus. She turns and waves. You arrive 5 minutes early and cheerfully greet the staff. Your boss comments on how good the day you are having. Notice the difference? Two different scenarios. Both started the same. Both ended differently. Why? Because of how you REACTED. You do not have any control over 10% of what happens. The other 90% was determined by your reaction. Here are some ways to apply the 90/10 principle. If someone says something negative about you, don't be a sponge. Let the attack roll off like water on glass. You don't have to let the negative comment affect you! React properly and it will not ruin your day. A wrong reaction could result in losing a friend, being fired, getting stressed out, etc. How do you react if someone cuts you off in traffic? Do you lose your temper? Pound on the steering wheel? A friend of mine had the steering wheel fall off) Do you curse? Does your blood pressure skyrocket? Do you try and bump them? WHO CARES if you arrive ten seconds later at work? Why let the cars ruin your drive? Remember the 90/10 principle, and do not worry about it. You are told you lost your job. Why lose sleep and get irritated? It will work out. Use your worrying energy and time to find another job. The plane is late; it is going to mangle your schedule for the day. Why take outpour frustration on the flight attendant? She has no control over what is going on. Use your time to study, and get to know the other passengers. Why get stressed out? It will just make things worse. Now you know the 90-10 principle. Apply it and you will be amazed at the results. You will lose nothing if you try it. The 90-10 principle is incredible. Very few know and apply this principle. The result?

Life Lessons: Millions of people are suffering from undeserved stress, trials, problems, and heartache. We all must understand and apply the 90/10 principle. It CAN change your life!!! Enjoy...

8. Sunflower

A family moved into their new home some years ago and they spent a lot of time and energy in the yard to make it look green. They lived on a corner, higher than street level, and the entire side of the yard was encased by a professionally built rock wall. They did their best and changed that area to their 'rock garden'. Last summer they found a tiny little plant at the end of the rock garden that they could not immediately identify. They knew that they didn't plant it. They decided to let it continue growing until they could figure out what it was. Weeks passed and as they made their way back to the mystery plant, it appeared to be a Sunflower. It was spindly looking with a tall skinny stalk and only one head on it. They decided to baby it along and weed around it. As they pulled rocks from the area to get to the weeds, they noticed something unusual. The Sunflower had not started where they saw the stalk begin. It had begun under a big rock and grown under and around it to reach the sun. This makes us realize that if a tiny little Sunflower didn't let a big rock stand in its way of developing, we too have the capability of doing the same thing. Once our environment begins to see that we believe in ourselves like that little Sunflower, we can attain the same nourishment and nurturing as well. First, we need to believe in ourselves knowing we have the capabilities in achieving our desires. Like the Sunflower, it knew it had the capability to overcome its obstacle because it trusted in the Universal Truth and had faith it would succeed.

Life Lessons: Stand tall like the Sunflower and be proud of who and what you are and the environment will begin to support you. You will find a way to go under or around your big obstacle in order to reach your desires.

9. Sand and Stones

A story tells that two friends were walking through the desert. During some point in the journey, they had an argument, and one friend slapped the other one in the face. The one who got slapped was hurt, but without saying anything, wrote in the sand: "TODAY MY BEST FRIEND SLAPPED ME IN THE FACE." They kept on walking until they found an oasis, where they decided to take a bath. The one, who had been slapped, got stuck in the mire and started drowning, but the friend saved him. After the friend recovered from the near drowning, he wrote on a stone: "TODAY MY BEST FRIEND SAVED MY

LIFE." The friend who had slapped and saved his best friend asked him, "After I hurt you, you wrote in the sand and now, you write on a stone, why?" The other friend replied: "When someone hurts us, we should write it down in sand where winds of forgiveness can erase it away. But, when someone does something good for us, we must engrave it in stone where no wind can ever erase it."

Life Lessons: Learn to write your hurts in the sand, and to carve your benefits in stone

10. Poison in mind

A long time ago in China, a girl named Li-Li got married & went to live with her husband and mother-in-law. In a very short time, Li-Li found that she couldn't get along with her mother-in-law at all. Their personalities were very different, and Li-Li was anger red by many of her mother-in-law's habits. In addition, she criticized Li-Li Constantly. Days passed, and weeks passed. Li-Li and her mother-in-law never stopped arguing and fighting. But what made the situation even worse was that, according to ancient Chinese tradition, Li-Li had to bow to her mother-in-law and obey her every wish. All the anger and unhappiness in the house was causing Li-Li's poor husband great distress. Finally, Li-Li could not stand her mother-in-law's bad temper and dictatorship any longer, and she decided to do something about it! Li-Li went to see her father's good friend, Mr. Huang, who sold herbs. She told him the situation and asked if he would give her some poison so that she could solve the problem once and for all. Mr. Huang thought for a while, and finally said, "Li-Li, I will help you solve your problem, but you must listen to me and obey what I tell you." Li-Li said, "Yes, Mr. Huang, I will do whatever you tell me to do." Mr. Huang went into the back room and returned in a few minutes with a package of herbs. He told Li-Li, "You can't use a quick-acting poison to get rid of your mother-in-law, because that would cause people to become suspicious. Therefore, I have given you a number of herbs that will slowly build up poison in her body. Every other day prepares some delicious meal and puts a little of these herbs in her serving. Now, in order to make sure that nobody suspects you. When she dies, you must be very careful to act very friendly towards her. "Don't argue with her, obey her every wish, and treat her like a queen." Li-Li was so happy. She thanked Mr. Huang and hurried home to start her plot of murdering her mother-in-law. Weeks went by, and months went by, and every other day, Li-Li served the specially treated food to her mother-in-law. She remembered what Mr. Huang ha d said about avoiding suspicion, so she controlled her temper, obeyed her mother-in-law, and treated her like her own mother. After six months had passed, the whole household had changed. Li-Li had practiced controlling her temper so much that she found that she almost never got mad or upset. She hadn't had an argument with her mother-in-law in six months because she now seemed much kinder and easier to get along with. The mother-in-law's attitude toward Li-Li changed, and she began to love Li-Li is like her own daughter. She kept telling friends and relatives that Li-Li was the best daughter-in-law one could ever find. Li-Li and her mother-in-law were now treating each other like a real mother and daughter. Li-Li's husband was very happy to see what was happening. One day, Li-Li came to see Mr. Huang and asked for his help again. She said, "Dear Mr. Huang, please help me to keep the poison from killing my mother-in-law! She's changed into such a nice woman, and I love her like my own mother. I do not want her to die because of the poison I gave her." Mr. Huang smiled and nodded his head. "Li-Li, there's nothing to worry about. I never gave you any poison. The herbs I gave you were vitamins to improve her health. The only poison was in your mind and your attitude toward her, but that has been all washed away by the love which you gave to her." HAVE YOU REALIZED that how you treat others is exactly how they will treat you? There is a wise Chinese saying: "The person who loves others will also be loved in return."

Life Lessons: Give the same treatment from others that you expect from them.

11. God's Coffee

A group of alumni, highly established in their careers, got together to visit their old university professor. Conversation soon turned into complaints about stress in work and life. Offering his guests coffee, the professor went to the kitchen and returned with a large pot of coffee and an assortment of cups - porcelain, plastic, glass, crystal, some plain looking, some expensive, some exquisite - telling them to help themselves to the coffee. When all the students had a cup of coffee in hand, the professor said: "If you noticed, all the nice looking expensive cups were taken up, leaving behind the plain and cheap ones. While it is normal for you to want only the best for yourselves, that is the source of your problems and stress. Be assured that the cup itself adds no quality to the coffee. In most cases it is just more expensive and, in some cases, even hides what we drink. What all of you really wanted was coffee, not the cup, but you consciously went for the best cups... And then you began eyeing each other's cups. Now consider this: Life is the coffee; the jobs, money and position in society are the cups. They are just tools to hold and contain Life, and the type of cup we have does not define, nor change the quality of Life we live. Sometimes, by concentrating only on the cup, we fail to enjoy the coffee God has provided us." God brews the coffee, not the cups.......... Enjoy your coffee! "The happiest people don't have the best of everything. They just make the best of everything."

Life Lessons: Live simply. Love generously. Care deeply. Speak kindly. Leave the rest to God. May We'll be able to Relish All the Coffees of our lives..!

12. Potatoes

A kindergarten teacher has decided to let her class play a game. The teacher told each child in the class to bring along a plastic bag containing a few potatoes. Each potato will be given the name of a person that the child hates, so the number of potatoes that a child will put in his/her plastic bag will depend on the number of people he/she hates. So when the day came, every child bought some potatoes with the name of the people he/she hated. Some had 2 potatoes; some 3 while some up to 5 potatoes. The teacher then told the children to carry with them the potatoes in the plastic bag whenever they went (even to the toilet) for one week. Days after days passed by, and they started to complain due to the unpleasant smell let out by the rotten potatoes. Besides, those given 5 potatoes also had to carry heavier bags. After 1 week, the children were relieved because the game had finally ended. The teacher asked: "How did you feel while carrying the potatoes with u for 1 week?" the children let out their frustration and started complaining about the trouble that they had to go through having to carry the heavy and smelly potatoes whenever they go. Then the teacher told them the hidden meaning behind the game. The teacher said: "This is exactly the situation when you carry your hatred for somebody inside your heart. The stench of hatred will contaminate your heart and you will carry it with you whenever you go. If you cannot tolerate the smell of rotten potatoes for just 1 week, can you imagine what is it like to have the stench of hatred in your heart for your lifetime???"

Life Lessons : Throw away any hatred for anyone from your heart so that you will not carry sins for a lifetime. Forgiving others is the best attitude to take!

13. Never Lose Your Value

A well-known speaker started off his seminar by holding up a $500/- note in the room of 200, He asked, "Who would like this 500 note?" Hands started going up. He said, "I am going to give this note to one of you but first let me do this." He proceeded to crumple the note up. He then asked, "Who still wants it?" Still, the hands were up in the air. "Well," he replied, "What if I do this?" And he dropped it on the ground and started to grind it into the floor with his shoe. He picked it up, now all crumpled and dirty. "Now who still wants it?" Still, the hands went into the air. "My friends, you have all learned a very valuable Lesson. No matter what I did to the money, you still wanted it because it did not decrease in value. It was still worth $ 500/-. Many times, in our lives, we are dropped, crumpled, and ground into the dirt by the decisions we make and the circumstances that come our way. We feel as though we are worthless. But no matter what has happened or what will happen, you will never lose your value. You are special don't ever forget it!

Life Lessons : Never let yesterday's disappointments overshadow tomorrow's dreams.

14. A wedding gift

She married him today. At the end of the wedding party, her mother gave her a newly opened bank savings passbook, with $1000 deposited in it. She told her, "My dear daughter, take this passbook. Keep it as a record of your married life. Whenever something happy and memorable happens in your new life, put some money in. Write down what it's about next to the amount. The more memorable the event is, the more money you can put in. I've done the first one for you today. Do the others with your husband. When you look back after many years, you will know how much happiness you've both shared.' She shared this with him after getting home. Both of them thought it was a great idea and couldn't wait to make the next deposit! This is what the passbook looked like after a while: - 7 Feb: $100, his first birthday celebration after marriage 1 Mar: $300, she gets a salary raise 20 Mar: $200, vacation 15 Apr: $2000, She's pregnant! 1 Jun: $1000, He gets the big promotion and so on... However, as the years went by, they began fighting and arguing over trivial things. They didn't talk much. They regretted that they had married the nastiest person in the world. There was no more love. One day she talked to her mother. 'Mom, we can't stand it anymore. We have decided to divorce. I can't imagine how I decided to marry this guy!' Her mother replied, 'Sure, that's no big deal. Just do whatever you want, if you really can't stand it. But before that, do one thing remember the savings passbook I gave you on your wedding day? Take out all the money and spend it first. You shouldn't keep any record of such a poor marriage.' She agreed with her mother. So she went to the bank and was waiting in the queue to cancel the account. While she was waiting, she took a look at the passbook record. She looked and looked, and looked. Then the memory of all the previous joyful moments came back to her. Her eyes were filled with tears. She left and went home. When she got home, she handed the passbook to her hubby and asked him to spend the money before getting divorced. So the next day, he went to the bank and was waiting in the queue to cancel the account. While he was waiting, he took a look at the passbook record. He looked and looked, and looked. Then the memory of all the previous joyful moments came back to him. His eyes were filled with tears. He left and went home. He gave the passbook back to her. She found a new deposit of $5000.

And a line next to the record: 'This is the day I realized how much I've loved you throughout all these years. How much happiness you've brought me.' They hugged and cried, putting the passbook back into the safe.

Life Lessons: Marriage is not a game, it's not easy but it's beautiful. You will fight and argue, this is normal, because both of you came from different backgrounds and different homes, and you both were raised by different parents, beliefs, and morals. So you cannot expect that everything you say will be accepted by your spouse without their opinion being tendered first. So before you give up, think back to the good times and to what brought you together in the first place. Dedicated to all married couples.

15. Integrity

A successful businessman was growing old and knew it was time to choose a successor to take over the business. Instead of choosing one of his Directors or his children, he decided to do something different. He called all the young executives in his company together. He said, "It is time for me to step down and choose the next CEO. I have decided to choose one of you."The young executives were Shocked, but the boss continued. "I am going to give each one of you a SEED today – one very special SEED... I want you to plant the seed, water it, and come back here one year from today with what you have grown from the seed I have given you. I will then judge the plants that you bring, and the one I choose will be the next CEO." One man, named Jim, was there that day and he, like the others, received a seed. He went home and excitedly told his wife the story. She helped him get a pot, soil, and compost and he planted the seed. Every day, he would water it and watch to see if it had grown. After about three weeks, some of the other executives began to talk about their seeds and the plants that were beginning to grow. Jim kept checking his seed, but nothing ever grew. Three weeks, four weeks, five weeks went by, and still nothing. By now, others were talking about their plants, but Jim didn't have a plant and he felt like a failure. Six months went by — still nothing in Jim's pot. He just knew he had killed his seed. Everyone else had trees and tall plants, but he had nothing. Jim didn't say anything to his colleagues, however. He just kept watering and fertilizing the soil – He so wanted the seed to grow. A year finally went by and all the young executives of the company brought their plants to the CEO for inspection. Jim told his wife that he wasn't going to take an empty pot. But she asked him to be honest about what happened. Jim felt sick to his stomach, it was going to be the most embarrassing moment of his life, but he knew his wife was right. He took his empty pot to the board room. When Jim arrived, he was amazed at the variety of plants grown by the other executives. They were beautiful — in all shapes and sizes. Jim put his empty pot on the floor and many of his colleagues laughed, a few felt sorry for him! When the CEO arrived, he surveyed the room and greeted his young executives. Jim just tried to hide in the back. "My, what great plants, trees, and flowers you have grown," said the CEO. "Today one of you will be appointed the next CEO!" All of a sudden, the CEO spotted Jim at the back of the room with his empty pot. He ordered the Financial Director to bring him to the front. Jim was terrified. He thought, "The CEO knows I'm a failure! Maybe he will have me fired!" When Jim got to the front, the CEO asked him what had happened to his seed – Jim told him the story. The CEO asked everyone to sit down except Jim. He looked at Jim, and then announced to the young executives, "Behold your next Chief Executive Officer! His name is Jim!" Jim couldn't believe it. Jim couldn't even grow his seed. "How could he be the new CEO?" the others said. Then the CEO said, "One year ago today, I gave everyone in this room a seed. I told you to take the seed, plant it, water it, and bring it back to me today. But I gave you all boiled seeds; they were dead – it was not possible for them to grow. All of you, except Jim, have brought me trees and plants and flowers. When you found that the seed would not grow, you substituted another seed for the one I gave you. Jim was the only one with the courage and honesty to bring me a pot with my seed in it. Therefore, he is the one who will be the new Chief Executive Officer!" If you plant honesty, you will reap trust, If you plant goodness, you will reap friends, If you plant humility, you will reap greatness, If you plant perseverance, you will reap contentment, If you plant consideration, you will reap perspective, If you plant hard work, you will reap success, If you plant forgiveness, you will reap reconciliation, If you plant faith in God, you will reap a harvest. So, be careful what you plant now; it will determine what you will reap later.

Life Lessons : "Whatever You Give To Life, Life Gives You Back"

16. The Story of a Woodcutter

Once upon a time, a woodcutter got a job as a timber merchant. The merchant paid great incentive for bringing more trees, and so the woodcutter was determined to do his best. The merchant gave him an axe and showed him the area where he had to do his best. The first day the woodcutter brought 18 trees. The merchant said congratulations...way to go. Very motivated by his words, the woodcutter tried harder the next day, he could only bring 15 trees. The third day he tried even harder, but he could only bring 10 trees. Day after day he was bringing fewer and fewer trees. The Woodcutter thought, 'I must be losing my strength'. He went to the merchant and apologetically said "I don't know what is going on". The merchant asked "When was the last time you sharpened your axe?" Sharpen?? I had no time to sharpen my axe. I have been very busy cutting trees.

Life Lessons: Our lives are like that. We sometimes get so busy that we don't take the time to sharpen the "AXE". In today's world, it seems that everyone is busier than ever, but less happy than ever.

17. How heavy is a glass of water?

A lecturer, when explaining stress management to an audience, raised a glass of water and asked, "How heavy is this glass of water?" Answers called out ranged from 20g to 500g. The lecturer replied, "The absolute weight doesn't matter. It depends on how long you try to hold it." "If I hold it for a minute, that's not a problem. If I hold it for an hour, I'll have an ache in my right arm. If I hold it for a day, you'll have to call an ambulance. In each case, it's the same weight, but the longer I hold it, the heavier it becomes." He continued, "And that's the way it is with stress management. If we carry our burdens all the time, sooner or later, as the burden becomes increasingly heavy, we won't be able to carry on." "As with the glass of water, you have to put it down for a while and rest before holding it again. When we're refreshed, we can carry on with the burden." "So, before you return home tonight, put the burden of work down. Don't carry it home. You can pick it up tomorrow. Whatever burdens you're carrying now, let them down for a moment if you can." "Relax; pick them up later after you've rested. Life is yours. Enjoy it! **Life Lessons:** Overthinking is the biggest cause of unhappiness. Relieve yourself from stress and enjoy life.

18. Change our vision...!!

There was a millionaire who was bothered by severe eye pain. He consulted so many physicians and was getting his treatment done. He did not stop consulting a galaxy of medical experts; he consumed heavy loads of drugs and underwent hundreds of injections. But the ache persisted with greater vigor than before. At last a monk who was supposed to; be an expert in treating such patients was called for by the millionaire. The monk understood his problem and said that for some time he should concentrate only on green colors and not to fall his eyes on any other colors. The millionaire got together a group of painters and purchased barrels of green color and directed that every object his eye was likely; to fall to be painted in green color just as the monk had directed. When the monk came to visit him after a few days, the millionaire's servants ran with buckets of green paints and poured them on him since he was in a red dress, lest their master not see any other color and his eye ache would come back. Hearing this monk laughed and said "If only you had purchased a pair of green spectacles, worth just a few rupees, you could have saved these walls and trees and pots and all other articles and also could have saved a large share of his fortune.

Life Lessons: You cannot paint the world green." Let us change our vision and the world will appear accordingly. It is foolish to shape the world, let us shape ourselves first. Let's change our vision...!!

19. Positive talk

A man was lost while driving through the countryside. As he tried to reach for the map, he accidentally drove off the road into a ditch. Though he wasn't injured, his car was stuck deep in the mud. So the man walked to a nearby farm to ask for help. "Warwick can get you out of that ditch," said the farmer, pointing to an old mule standing in a field. The man looked at the decrepit old mule and looked at the farmer who just stood there repeating, "Yep, old Warwick can do the job." The man figured he had nothing to lose. The two men and the mule made their way back to the ditch. The farmer hitched the mule to the car. With a snap of the reins, he shouted, "Pull, Fred! Pull, Jack! Pull, Ted! Pull, Warwick!" And the mule pulled that car right out of the ditch. The man was amazed. He thanked the farmer, patted the mule, and asked, "Why did you call out all of those names before you called Warwick?" The farmer grinned and said, "Old Warwick is just about blind. As long as he believes he's part of a team, he doesn't mind pulling." Keep your words positive, because your words become your actions. Keep your actions positive, because your actions become your habits. Keep your habits positive, because your habits become your lifestyle. Keep your lifestyle positive, because your lifestyle becomes your destiny.

Life Lessons : Be Optimistic and all your dreams will come true.

20. Funeral

One day all the employees of a very unusual company reached their office and all saw a big sign on the main door which said this: "Yesterday, the person who has been hindering your growth in this company passed away. We invite you to join the funeral in the room that has been prepared in the gym." In the beginning, they all got sad for the death of one of their colleagues, but after a while they started getting curious to know who was that person who hindered the growth of their colleagues and the company itself? The excitement in the gym was such that security agents were ordered to control the crowd within the room. The more people reached the coffin, the more the excitement heated up. Everyone thought - "Who is this person who was hindering my progress?" One by one the intrigued employees got closer to the coffin, and when they looked inside it, they suddenly became speechless. They all got to stand near the coffin, and all ended up shocked and in silence as if someone had touched the deepest part of their soul. There was a mirror inside the coffin: everyone who looked inside it could see themselves! There was also a sign next to the mirror that said: There is only one person who is capable of setting limits to your growth and IT IS YOU! Your life does not change when your boss changes, when your friends change, when your parents change, when your husband or wife changes, when your company changes, when your church changes, when your location changes, when your money changes, when your status changes. No, your life changes when YOU change, when you go beyond your limiting beliefs.

Life Lessons : Examine yourself, watch yourself. Don't be afraid of difficulties, impossibilities, and losses. Be a winner; build yourself and your reality. It's the way you face life itself that makes the difference.

21. Baby Eagles

A long time ago, a king received 2 beautiful baby eagles in the form of a present. The king was very pleased with the gift & decided to hire an experienced caretaker for them. He took great care of them and developed such a strong bond with those two that they didn't need to be caged. After a few months, the king decided to visit them. He noticed that the two Babies had now developed into strong adolescents. The king wished to see them flying and ordered the caretaker to signal them to fly into the sky. On receiving his signal, both eagles began to fly. One of them flew high into the sky and touched new heights, while the other one flew for some seconds and returned to the branch where it was earlier sitting. King found this a little weird and asked the caretaker why these 2 are so contrasting. The caretaker told the king that this one had a problem from the beginning and he would never leave the branch. The king desperately wanted the second bird to fly as high as the first one. So he announced this as a challenge in his court and stated that the person who was successful in making the eagle fly would receive a heavy prize from the king. So, many scholars came and tried to apply the knowledge they had, but no one was successful. The king too lost hope and almost gave up. But after a few days, the caretaker informed the king that one man was successful in making the eagle fly high in the sky. He was then brought before the king where the king was eagerly waiting with the promised prize. The king learned that the man was a simple farmer. He just asked him what method he used which a lot of highly qualified people didn't think about. He said, "I simply cut the branch. The branch on which he had a habit of sitting. As there was no branch, he had no option but to fly. And which he did very well."

Life Lessons : We all are meant to fly high in our lives. But sometimes we underestimate ourselves and don't realize our true potential. We are habituated to doing certain things which will always limit us. Just as the eagle didn't realize that it could fly as high as it always liked to remain on the branch. After the farmer had cut it, it had no option but to come out of its comfort zone and start working. Only then did he realize its true potential. Even we need to come out of our comfort zones as great things in life are only achieved out of the comfort zone in which we keep living and hoping for life to get better.

22. Don't Change the World

Once upon a time, there was a king who ruled a prosperous country. One day, he went on a trip to some distant areas of his country. When he was back to his palace, he complained that his feet were very painful, because it was the first time that he went for such a long trip, and the road that he went through was very rough and stony. He then ordered his people to cover every road in the entire country with leather. This would need thousands of cows' skin and would cost a huge amount of money. Then one of his wise servants dared himself to tell the king, "Why do you have to spend that unnecessary amount of money? Why don't you just cut a little piece of leather to cover your feet?" The king was surprised, but he later agreed to his suggestion, to make a "shoe" for himself.

Life Lessons : To make this world a happy place to live, you better change yourself - your heart; and not the world.

23. Your temper

There was a little boy with a bad temper. His father gave him a bag of nails and told him that every time he lost his temper, he should hammer a nail in the back fence. On the first day, the boy had driven 37 nails into the fence. Then it gradually dwindled. He discovered it was easier to hold his temper than to drive those nails into the fence. Finally, the day came when the boy didn't lose his temper at all. He told his father about it and the father suggested that the boy now pull out one nail for each day that he was able to hold his temper. The days passed and the young boy was finally able to tell his father that all the nails were gone. The father took his son by the hand and led him to the fence. He said, "You have done well, my son, but look at the holes in the fence. The fence will never be the same. When you say things in anger, they leave a scar just like this one. You can put a knife in a man and draw it out. It won't matter how many times you say" I'm sorry," but the wound will still be there. A verbal wound is even worse than a physical one.

Life Lessons : When you are angry....... You lose more than your temper. Always remember, Anger is just a 'D' short of Danger.

24. Two Frogs

A group of frogs were traveling through the woods, and two of them fell into a deep pit. When the other frogs saw how deep the pit was, they told the two frogs that they were as good as dead. The two frogs ignored the comments and tried to jump up out of the pit with all their might. The other frogs kept telling them to stop, that they were as good as dead. Finally, one of the frogs took heed to what the other frogs were saying and gave up. He fell down and died. The other frog continued to jump as hard as he could. Once again, the crowd of frogs yelled at him to stop the pain and just die. He jumped even harder and finally made it out. When he got out, the other frogs said, "Did you not hear us?" The frog explained to them that he was deaf. He thought they were encouraging him the entire time. 1. There is power of life and death in the tongue. An encouraging word to someone who is down can lift them and help them make it through the day. 2. A destructive word to someone who is down can be what it takes to kill them. Be careful of what you say. Speak life to those who cross your path.

Life Lessons : The power of words. It is sometimes hard to understand that an encouraging word can go such a long way. Anyone can speak words that tend to rob another of the spirit to continue in difficult times. Special is the individual who will take the time to encourage another.

25. A glass of milk

One day, a poor boy who was selling goods from door to door to pay his way through school, found he had only one thin dime left, and he was hungry. He decided he would ask for a meal at the next house. However, he lost his nerve when a lovely young woman opened the door. Instead of a meal he asked for a drink of water. She thought he looked hungry so brought him a large glass of milk. He drank it slowly, and then asked, "How much do I owe you?" "You don't owe me anything," she replied. "Mother has taught us never to accept payment for kindness." He said..... "Then I thank you from my heart." As the boy left that house, he not only felt stronger physically, but his faith in God and man was strong also. Years later that young woman became critically ill. The local doctors were baffled. They finally sent her to the big city, where they called in specialists to study her rare disease. The boy who was now a Doctor was named Dr. Howard Kelly was called in for the consultation. When he heard the name of the town she came from, a strange light filled his eyes. Immediately he rose and went down the hall of the hospital to her room. Dressed in his doctor's gown he went in to see her. He recognized her at once. He went back to the consultation room determined to do his best to save her life. From that day he gave special attention to the case.

Life Lessons : Be kind and help the needy without any expectation. Someday it will come back to you in unexpected ways.

26. Level of Confidence

Story told by a man which is the most frightening yet thought-provoking experience of his life. He had been on a long flight. The first warning of the approaching problems came when the sign on the airplane flashed: "Fasten your seat belts." Then, after a while, a calm voice said, "We shall not be serving the beverages at this time as we are expecting a little turbulence. Please be sure your seat belt is fastened." As he looked around the aircraft, it became obvious that many of the passengers were becoming apprehensive. Later, the voice of the announcer said, "We are so sorry that we are unable to serve the meal at this time. The turbulence is still ahead of us." And then the storm broke. The ominous cracks of thunder could be heard even above the roar of the engines. Lightening lit up the darkening skies and within moments that great plane was like a cork tossed around on a celestial ocean. One moment the airplane was lifted on terrific currents of air; the next, it dropped as if it were about to crash. The man confessed that he shared the discomfort and fear of those around him. He said, "As I looked around the plane, I could see that nearly all the passengers were upset and alarmed. Some were praying. The future seemed ominous and many were wondering if they would make it through the storm. And then, I suddenly saw a girl to whom the storm meant nothing. She had tucked her feet beneath her as she sat on her seat and was reading a book. Everything within her small world was calm and orderly. Sometimes she closed her eyes, then she would read again; then she would straighten her legs, but worry and fear were not in her world. When the plane was being buffeted by the terrible storm, when it lurched this way and that, as it rose and fell with frightening severity, when all the adults were scared half to death, that marvellous child was completely composed and unafraid." The man could hardly believe his eyes. It was not surprising therefore, that when the plane finally reached its destination and all the passengers were hurrying to disembark, he lingered to speak to the girl whom he had watched for such a long time. Having commented about the storm and the behavior of the plane, he asked why she had not been afraid. The sweet child replied, "Sir, my Dad is the pilot and he is taking me home."

Life Lessons : When you have confidence and trust in yourself as well as near ones around you, you will face all the challenges of your life successfully.

27. Give Cent Percent

A boy and a girl were playing together. The boy had a collection of marbles. The girl had some sweets with her. The boy told the girl that he would give her all his marbles in exchange for her sweets. The girl agreed. The boy kept the biggest and the most beautiful marble aside and gave the rest to the girl. The girl gave him all her sweets as she had promised. That night, the girl slept peacefully. But the boy couldn't sleep as he kept wondering if the girl had hidden some sweets from him the way he had hidden his best marble.

Life Lessons : If you don't give your hundred percent in a relationship, you'll always keep doubting whether the other person has given his/her hundred percent or not. So, for any relationship, give your hundred percent to everything you do and enjoy.

28. Know the Rose Within yourself

A certain man planted a rose and watered it faithfully and before it blossomed, he examined it. He saw the bud that would soon blossom but noticed thorns upon the stem and he thought, "How can any beautiful flower come from a plant burdened with so many sharp thorns? Saddened by this thought, he neglected to water the rose, and just before it was ready to bloom... it died. So it is with many people. Within every soul, there is a rose. The God-like qualities planted in us at birth, grow amid the thorns of our faults. Many of us look at ourselves and see only the thorns, the defects. We despair, thinking that nothing good can come from us. We neglect to water the good within us, and eventually, it dies. We never realize our potential. Some people do not see the rose within themselves; someone else must show it to them. One of the greatest gifts a person can possess is to be able to reach past the thorns of another and find the rose within them. This is one of the characteristics of love... to look at a person, know their true faults, and accept that person into your life... all the while recognizing the nobility in their soul.

Life Lessons : Help others to realize they can overcome their faults. If we show them the "rose" within themselves, they will conquer their thorns. Only then will they blossom many times over.

29. Don't work but Serve

One evening a Swamiji of Sri Ramakrishna Mutt was addressing the participants of an MNC company on the concept of work culture. One of the participants asked the following question Swamiji: I am a senior manager of the Materials Department and I joined an organization 25 years ago as an Engineer Trainee. Over the last 25 years I have gone through every experience in the organization and I am now the senior manager looking after the material function independently. During the initial part of my career, the job was very challenging and interesting. Every day was exciting and I looked forward to each day with a lot of interest. However, all those exciting days are gone since I do not find my job any more interesting because there is nothing new in my job. As I have seen and handled every conceivable situation there are no more challenges in my work. I am now feeling bored because I am doing a routine job. However, Swamiji, I have been living in the same house for over forty years, I am the son of the same parents for over forty-five years, I am the father of the same children for the past ten years and the husband for the same lady for the past twenty years. In these personal roles, I do not feel bored and the passage of time has not taken away the zeal from me. Please tell me why I am bored of the routine in the office and not in the house. This was a very interesting question and we were all very anxious and curious to know what the Swamiji had to say. The response from him was very interesting and convincing. He asked the executive the question: Please tell me for whom does your wife and the mother of children cook? The executive replied that obviously, my wife cooks for all of us -the family. Then the Swamiji said that because the wife 'Serves' others and because of this service mindedness, she is not feeling tired or bored. Similarly, when you are at Home you do not perceive your role as the necessary work. But in an office, we 'Work' and not 'Serve'. Anything we consider, as service, will not make us feel bored. That is the difference between Serving and Working. He asked the executive to consider his work as service and not merely work.

Life Lessons: If you love what you do, then you will never feel bored.

30. The Wooden Bowl

A frail old man went to live with his son, daughter-in-law, and a four-year-old grandson. The old man's hands trembled, his eyesight was blurred, and his step faltered. The family ate together every night at the dinner table. But the elderly grandfather's shaky hands and failing sight made eating rather difficult. Peas rolled off his spoon onto the floor. When he grasped the glass often milk spilled on the tablecloth. The son and daughter-in-law became irritated with the mess. "We must do something about grandfather," said the son. I've had enough of his spilled milk, noisy eating, and food on the floor. So the husband and wife set a small table in the corner. There, grandfather ate alone while the rest of the family enjoyed dinner at the dinner table. Since grandfather had broken a dish or two, his food was served in a wooden bowl. Sometimes when the family glanced in grandfather's direction, he had a tear in his eye as he ate alone. Still, the only words the couple had for him were sharp admonitions when he dropped a fork or spilled food. The four-year-old watched it all in silence. One evening before supper, the father noticed his son playing with wood scraps on the floor. He asked the child sweetly, "What are you making?" Just as sweetly, the boy responded, "Oh, I am making a little bowl for you and mama to eat your food from when I grow up." The four-year-old smiled and went back to work. The words so struck the parents that they were speechless. Then tears started to stream down their cheeks. Though no word was spoken, both knew what must be done. That evening the husband took grandfather's hand and gently led him back to the family table. For the remainder of his days, he ate every meal with the family. And for some reason, neither husband nor wife seemed to care any longer when a fork was dropped, milk spilled, or the tablecloth soiled. Children are remarkably perceptive. Their eyes ever observe, their ears ever listen, and their minds ever process the messages they absorb. If they see us patiently providing a happy home atmosphere for family members, they will imitate that attitude for the rest of their lives. The wise parent realizes that every day building blocks are being laid for the child's future. Let us all be wise builders and role models.

Life Lessons : Take care of yourself, and those you love... today, and every day!

31. SHOUT

A saint asked his disciples, 'Why do we shout in anger? Why do people shout at each other when they are upset?' His disciples thought for a while, and one of them said, 'Because we lose our calm, we shout for that.' 'But, why do you shout when the other person is just next to you?' asked the saint. 'Isn't it possible to speak to him or her with a soft voice? Disciples gave some other answers but none satisfied the saint. Finally, he explained, 'When two people are angry at each other, their hearts distance a lot.

To cover that distance, they must shout to be able to hear each other. The angrier they are, the stronger they will have to shout to hear each other through that great distance.' Then the saint asked, 'What happens when two people fall in love? They don't shout at each other but talk softly, why? Because their hearts are very close. The distance between them is very small...' The saint continued, 'When they love each other even more, what happens? They do not speak, only whisper and they get even closer to each other in their love. Finally, they need not whisper, they only look at each other and that's all. That is how close two people are when they love each other.

Life Lessons : When you argue, do not let your hearts get distant, do not say words that distance each other more, else there will come a day when the distance is so great that you will not find the path to return.

HOW TO HAVE A GOOD DAY	HOW TO HAVE A BAD DAY
Wake up early - don't rush Breath slowly and deeply Exercise	Wake up late, in a panic
	Rush to get ready
	Dress hurriedly
Take 5 minutes to reflect	Don't eat
Greet everyone	Drink lots of coffee
Smile a lot	No spiritual reflection
Compliment often	No exercise
Communicate	Don't plan your day
Listen more - talk less	Focus on your failures
Beware of giving advice	Never smile
View your work as a privilege Express appreciation	Be selfish and unfriendly
	Criticize, blame, complain
	Think negative thoughts
Do your best	Dictate, direct, command
Welcome change	Don't forget to nag

Relax your neck muscles Plan time for relaxation Throw away negative feelings Let go of anger and guilt Leave work at work Review your accomplishments Plan pleasurable events Eat well at night Recognize your blessings	Don't overlook mistakes Grumble No time for lunch Harborit resentment Keep rushing Don't communicate Keep it all to yourself Worry about tomorrow Be rigid and cranky Retire with bad thoughts and a full stomach

*****

4 : The Spiritual Journey

Spirituality helps a person to improve relationships with themselves, others, the supreme power and environment. It is an individual's search for the ultimate purpose of life. It is basically a journey of becoming the most beautiful and powerful form of yourself.

Let me take you on one such journey which I have experienced over a period of time.

4.1 Swadhyaya

During my school days, I was associated with the Swadhyay activities under the guidance of Shri Pandurang Athawale Shastriji who was fondly known as "Dada". Before sharing my experiences of Swadhyay activities, Let me first share with you the meaning of Swadhyay activities. Swadhyay means the study of self, understanding the self and thereby becoming a better human being. It is very important for an individual to know his/her strengths and weaknesses. And Dada was of the belief that one can practice Swadhyay by studying and understanding the lessons from Bhagavad Gita. He taught us the basic principles of Bhagavad Gita. In order to learn the Bhagavad Gita in a lucid manner, we used to watch the videos of Dada where he would talk about the different life lessons from the Bhagavad Gita Verse by Verse. This we used to do on a weekly basis. This Swadhyay helped us embark on the journey of becoming a better human being and enrich our lives for the better. Dada used to talk about different experiments for different class of people. Some of them are Amrutalayam, Balsanskar Kendra, Trikal Sandhya, Bhakti Feri, Yogeshwar Krushi. For intellectual development of students, there was a divine brain trust which is popularly known as DBT. DBT used to host monthly debates on a given topic which used to create a lot of insights about our spiritual knowledge as well as the journey. Dada always emphasized the fact and wanted us to imbibe a principle from Bhagavad Gita of " Doing without Expecting. He explained that you should do your karma without expecting anything in return. At some point of time you will definitely reap the benefits of your good karma. Trust in God was also one of the very important lessons from the Swadhyay activity. Dada taught us the art of developing intellectual love towards God and asked us to believe that God will take care of us in all respects and under all circumstances. He told us that Lord Krishna is at the centre of all our activities. For Example, while we are lighting the morning lamp, we should always pray that whatever activities I undertake today, God is at the centre. Keeping God in your mind continuously will lead you towards performing all your activities in a righteous manner without harming any creature on the earth.

4.2   *Yoga Abhyas*

In the second part of my spiritual journey, I would like to share my experience of becoming a Yoga Teacher.

During November, 2019, I got a chance to undergo extensive training for becoming a yoga teacher under the guidance of my Guruji, Dr Rakesh Giri. Learning Yoga played a huge role in enhancing my spiritual journey.

Let me start with the meaning of "Yoga"

Yoga karmasu kaushalam - It means excellence in any type of work.

Yoga is a journey of the self, through the self and to the self.

Yoga is the alignment of Mind, Body and Soul and to achieve this alignment there are eight types of Limbs of yoga.

The same are discussed below;

1. **Yama - Behaviour and Interaction with others.** The Sublimbs are;

a. **Ahimsa - Non – Violence**

    i.   Non- Violence towards your mind - Being judgemental about others, criticizing them, blaming them, gossiping about them.

    ii. Non - violence towards your body - Consuming alcohol, tobacco, junk food, excessive sugary food, tea, coffee, over exercising. So we should be non violent to both our mind and body.

b. **Asteya - Non Stealing.** As per Leo Tolstoy, the kingdom of God is within us. As per the Vedas "Aham Brahmasmi" - the universe is within you. We need to train ourselves to enjoy whatever we have rather than running after getting more and more. Whenever we feel inferior or small, we need to just recite "I am enough, I have enough". Contentment is a very important quality one needs to develop.

c. Satya - Truthfulness. It is about alignment in your thoughts, words and actions. Speaking lies will create a lot of disturbance in your mind and will create hindrances in performing your task authentically. Yoga Chitta Vrutti Nirodhi - It means yoga is the solution to disturbances in the mind.

d. Aparigraha Non possessiveness. We should cultivate a habit of not having more than necessary and keep only those things which are truly needed. Too much of anything is bad. We need not collect more and more things than we require.

e. Brahmacharya – Not having any desire. Being a part of Brahma and practicing moderation in whatever you do.

2.   **Niyama - Self discipline**. The sublimbs are;

a) **Saucha (Cleanliness)** - Purification of mind and body.

For purification of mind, we need to watch content that uplifts us, helps us learn and grow and keep a company where we don't gossip and be around motivating people

b) **Santosha (Contentment)** - Being contented in whatever you have.

We should not attach ourselves to external circumstances and always live in gratitude. We should try not to be a control freak and stop chasing things. The one you are chasing will always come back to you, once you relax towards the same.

c) **Tapas (Self - discipline / Asceticism)** - Practicing discipline in daily life along with willpower and utmost positivity

d) **Svadhyaya (Self - reflection)** - Understanding our strengths, weaknesses, skills, knowledge and ability.

e) **Ishwara Pranidhana (Surrender to higher power)** Seeking divinity in everything and everyone and developing an attitude of positivity towards a person, object or a situation. For Eg : When we greet people with Namaste, we are actually doing Namaste to the God residing in that person which is the sign of respecting the human being as well as the God residing in that human being.

3.   Asana - The Body Discipline - Posture

Sthiram Sukham Asana - Posture is the one which brings stability and stillness. It is a practice to remove toxins from our body. While doing asanas we achieve stillness and calmness in our body

4.   Pranayama - Breathing techniques

It is controlling and stabilizing our breathing technique. It is the inhalation and exhalation of breath with retention

5.   Pratyabharti - Sense discipline

It is about having control over our five senses which are eyes, nose, skin, ears and tongue. It means that we should always see good things, always hear good things, eat good things and keep ourselves away from sense gratification and related things. It says that the senses should try and observe only positive things in all the human beings and every situation

6.   Dharana - Focused concentration (Aim discipline)

It is about binding the mind to one place, object or idea. It is about focusing on self-awareness and achieving one pointedness and getting back to that one pointedness in case you lose the focus.

7.   Dhyana - Meditative absorption

It is about meditation with discipline. With Dhyana, new thoughts are developed that have an ability to heal our mind and body. When we are in meditation, without sleeping we can achieve focus. We can get lesser thoughts or no thoughts

8.   Samadhi   -   Self-realization,   Bliss, Enlightenment

Satt Chitta Anand - Truth, consciousness, bliss. It is about being not affected by environmental negativity, social events and related things and being in a state of happiness and bliss.

All the above discussed eight limbs called Ashtanga Yoga, will help a person gain alignment between mind, body and soul and enrich them in physically, mentally and emotionally

4.3   Learnings from Srimad Bhagavad Gita Mastery Course

Further I will be sharing my experience of undergoing a Srimad Bhagavad Gita mastery course online conducted by Iscon - Chennai under the guidance of Prabhu Amrendra Gaur and Mataji - Sukriti Madhavi during the Covid pandemic.

I developed multiple insights on Srimad Bhagavad Gita. I will be sharing six of them which are helpful to me in my daily life.

1. Human beings are different from animals. Animal life is eating, sleeping, meeting and defending and if we as human beings do the same thing we are no different from animals and hence we should try and do something different than animals.

2. There are three types of miseries that a human being experiences in his/her lifetime.
a) Adhyatmika - Miseries caused by mind and body like illness
b) Adhibandika - Miseries caused by society, community
c) Adhidaivika - Miseries cause by natural calamities like flood, cyclone,pandemic

Our body is of three types

a) Gross body - consists of earth, Fire, Water, Air, Ether
b) Subtle body - Consists of mind, intelligence, false ego
c) Spiritual body - Consists of soul

There are four classes of people

a) Brahmana - Intellectual class - teachers
b) Kshatriya - Administrators class
c) Shudras - Working class
d) Vaishya - Business class

Three modes of material nature

a) Sattva - Mode of Goodness - People in this category differentiate between right and wrong. Eg: Vibhishan from Ramayana who always worshipped God. These people eat satvik food.i.e. wholesome juicy food derived from nature. They always give respect to others, are not selfish, do not want self-glorification, are truthful, worthy and pleasing.
b) Raja -Mode of Passion - People in this category are intensely greedy, Self centered. Eg Ravana from Ramayana who always worshipped demons. These people eat hot, sour and bitter food. They always have selfish intentions, do not respect others, are manipulative, always anxious and dissatisfied.
c) Tama - Mode of Ignorance - People in this category have no control over their sleeping as well as eating habits. Eg Kumbhakaran from Ramayana who always worshipped demons. They eat Tasteless, Decomposed and Non- Vegetarian food. They are always power hungry, intend to destroy others, fraudulent, impure, unworthy.

We need to enrich our transcendental knowledge and go beyond materialistic world and gain spiritual knowledge from bonafide gurus and so in order to enhance our transcendental knowledge there are 4 regulative principles to be kept in mind and Navavidha bhakti - Nine Steps of Bhakti

The four regulative principles are

1. No Meat, No Intoxicating items, No Gambling, No Illicit Sex
2. Chanting the Maha Mantra - Hare Krishna, Hare Krishna, Krishna Krishna Hare Hare, Hare rama, Hare Rama, Rama Rama Hare Hare
3. Reading spiritual scriptures like Srimad Bhagavad Gita, Srimad Bhagavatam and Vedas
4. Association with positive people

Navavidha bhakti - Nine Steps of Bhakti are

1. Shravanam - Hearing the God with attention
2. Keertanam - Glorifying the supreme God
3. Smaranama - Remembering the God
4. Padasam - Serving the devotees of the God
5. Archanam - Worshipping the lotus feet of God
6. Vandanam -Singing /Offering a specific prayer/ Aarti to God
7. Dashyam - Serving the God
8. Sathyam - Being friendly to the God
9. Atmanivedan - Surrendering to the God

Further I learnt about Mind

Our mind can be either our friend or our enemy. A friendly mind will always support our decisions, follow our directions, enhance our progress, provide freedom, detach our sense gratification and will help us gain complete control over situations.

An enemy mind will lead to sinful desires, irritation, agitation, attach to sense gratification and corrupt values

We must ensure that our mind is our friend and not enemy and to do so we must follow four things - ABCD

- A - Association of positive people
- B - Reading Srimad Bhagavad Gita
- C - Chanting Maha Mantra
- D - Consuming Satvik Diet

*****

5 : The Traits and Value System

5.1 The Personality traits

I want to give meaning to my name that is reflected in my personality, attitude and behaviour and that will be a guide to my way forward. My name is "Jignesh" where in

J stands for Joy - I am a joyful person and always believe in spreading joy and happiness

I stands for Intelligent - I am an intelligent person and have used my intelligence in the right way at all the stages of my personal as well as professional life

G stands for Genius - I am a genius as I possess some exceptional as well as extraordinary skills

N stands for Nice - I am always nice to people around me

E stands for Empathetic - I am empathetic and always step in the shoes of others and try and understand their feelings

S stands for Smart - I am a smart person in all the aspects

H stands for Honest - I am a honest person who has always placed honesty on the top most priority in all my endeavors

5.2   The Core Values

Further based on my personality traits and based on my firm beliefs i strongly believe in certain values and have carried these values with me across my professional career as well as personal life

The same are as mentioned below

Care and concern - I always showcase care, concern, love and affection for my family, friends and all my associates in the corporate world

Integrity - I give a lot of significance to integrity. I always believe in truthfulness, authenticity and transparency and am a firm believer in loyalty and trustworthiness

Commitment - I am a man of commitment. Whatever I commit, I always honour it. My thoughts, actions and behaviour are always in alignment. Generally, There is a perception about HR people that there is always a gap between what they speak and how they act which is not always true in everyone's case and thus unlike this perception, my actions and words are always in alignment with one another. I always portray high degree of commitment in all my activities

Self-discipline - I believe in high standards as far as discipline is concerned. I respect people who follow rules and regulations and always try and live a disciplined life

Timelines - I believe in completing all the tasks on time. I believe that time is very valuable and I always try to complete my tasks in a timely manner. I always respect my time as well as others time

Decisive - I believe "No Decision" is more costly than "Wrong Decision". Wrong decisions can be corrected but not taking decisions can put things, situations, events and relationships to halt. So I always believe in taking quick and accurate decisions with logic and reasoning after gathering necessary facts, information and data. Honestly, in my life i have taken some wrong decisions and due to the same I had faced financial losses also but I learnt a lesson from that experience and made sure that I do not commit the same type of mistake in future

Action - I am an action oriented person. I always like to act on whatever decision I take. I don't like things to be kept on hold. I always believe that everything should be logically disposed of either way. I believe in taking action.

Gratitude - I strongly believe that we need to develop a sense of gratitude. We should be grateful and thankful to god for whatever he has given and be contented about the same. We should never be jealous about what others have and put ourselves in stress. We should develop a mind-set of abundance rather than a mind-set of scarcity. Every day for 10 minutes, we should develop a practice of journaling gratitude by writing down and expressing our gratitude towards God. Although I have not been able to do it regularly, now I have decided to do it daily.

Be in the state of Satta chitta ananda - Truth, Consciousness and Bliss

So these are my eight personal values which I firmly believe and always practice in my personal, social and professional activities and the same value system is always reflected in whatever work I do.

*****

6 : Way Forward

I don't believe in formal retirement. I will continue working throughout my life as far as my health permits. Basically, Now, I will not work for money as money will be secondary for me. Now I wish to contribute to all the strata of the society which includes higher secondary students, adolescents, undergraduates, post graduates, junior executives, mid executives and Sr executives in the corporate. My only aim will be to spread message about celebrating the Utsav called life. I would help people in making their life more meaningful, beautiful and useful and how they can contribute to society.

I will spread my knowledge about how one can be physically, mentally, intellectually and spiritually healthy and make more and more people aware about the power of yoga which is an ultimate key to a healthy life

I will make people aware about the ways and means of enriching their lives spiritually and add divinity to their life by spreading the message of Srimad Bhagavad Gita and lord Krishna there by ensuring a healthy environment in the society. I will let people understand the power of love, affection, gratitude, kindness and compassion towards everybody thereby helping them create and live in a society where everybody is there for each other and enjoy each other's company

I wish that I am able to fulfill a very optimistic dream of spreading happiness across all the stratas of the society by the above mentioned ways and means

I wish that all the sections of people as discussed above learn something from my experiences, thought process and values mentioned in the book and not only learn but they practice the same in their day to day lives and in case while practicing they face any challenges then i will always love to help them and will be available for them.

*****

7 : Conclusion

- ➤ I hope 13 episodes, 10 pearls of wisdom and 31 chhoti chhoti baatein really leaves a positive impact on your minds and adds on to your personal as well as professional lives

- ➤ The spiritual journey that includes Swadhyay, Yoga Abhyas and learnings from Srimad Bhagavad Gita helps you stay physically, intellectually, mentally and spiritually healthy

- ➤ I further recommend that everyone one needs to practice an appropriate or suitable kind of physical exercise on a daily basis for at least 35 to 40 minutes and all the forms of yoga and meditation is one of the best ways to do that as fitness is the need of the hour in modern times

- ➤ We should always try to be associated with good people and stay away from negativity. Reading a good book, literature, scriptures and keeping in contact with good people will enhance your positivity as well as productivity.

- ➤ Well, I have achieved a lot of success in my professional career but other than the episodes, pearls, chhoti chhoti baatein and values, I would like to share one more thing. Honestly there was a particular phase in my career, where I have switched jobs very frequently and it had come with its own disadvantages and so for corporate executives, I would like to suggest that you should not keep changing your jobs just for the sake of the salary. One should take the decision of changing a job very carefully after analysing all the pros and cons of that decision. I always believe that flowing water is better than water stuck in one place but if you are gaining growth in an organization with respect to roles and responsibilities, authority, designation, salary and the related aspects then it is better to stick to that organization and build a strong career there rather than switching the organization in the pursuit of salary and designation.

- Amongst all the organizations that I have worked for I will rate my association with CLP Power India Ltd and Reliance as the best ones. These organizations have added a lot of value to my professional career.

- I started my career in the year 1989 which is the same year when the legend Sachin Tendulkar started his career. I often share with my friends over laughter that me and the legend both have started our professional journey together and Sachin Tendulkar has always inspired me and has been a motivating factor for me to perform better and better in my career.

- I am a firm believer in the idea of SACHHIDANAND. It means with respect to whatever God has given to me and in whatever state I am currently in, I am in Bliss, I am in Ananda, I am happy and would always love to live in the stage of SACHHIDANAND.

- So I would conclude by mentioning that I am very happy and contented with whatever God has given to me based on my knowledge, skills and ability and will always pray to God to help me use these to best of my capacity thereby contributing to the society in a continuous and conscious way. Yes, this is the journey, I don't claim that I am doing 100 percent but I have understood it and I am on a path and will continue to move on this path of gratitude, kindness, compassion and helping human beings become more and more noble.

- ➢ I am so grateful for the life I have

- ➢ I am so grateful for all the people that I have in my life

- ➢ I am so grateful for this loving, beautiful, healthy body I have; that continues to get stronger everyday

- ➢ I am so grateful for the work I do now, for many are jobless

- ➢ I am so thankful that the universe is working for my greater good

- ➢ Thank You for giving me another chance to make my life better today

- ➢ I am beyond blessed that I woke up today many did not have this privilege

Gratitude Diaries

In my journey of more than three decades, I am fortunate to have worked with different organizations and multiple associates who have been instrumental in helping me shape my career by providing excellent learning opportunities and have added to my journey directly as well as indirectly. I want to express my heartfelt gratitude and sincere thanks to all of them and want to name a few of my seniors and colleagues whom I have always hold in high regards.

- ❖ Shri G G Patel at Zaverchand Gaekwad Limited

- ❖ Shri S. N Choksi and Shri Ashok Pathak at Jyoti Limited

- ❖ Shri N V Jaywant, Shri A G Kolatkar, Shri A P Patel, Shri N B Wadia, Shri R D Sapre, Shri C J D'couna, Shri J N Pathak and Ms Virbala Rishi at Lupin Laboratories Ltd

- ❖ Late Shri V V Bhat, Late Shri I T Bhatt, Late Shri H S Kohli, Shri D D sudame, Shri N k Gaur, Shri K V Doshi, Shri P L gaiekwad, Shri D U Desai, Shri S D Mehta, Shri Siddharth Dhar at Reliance Industries Ltd

- ❖ Shri Rajiv Mishra, Shri Anup Kundu, Shri Pankaj shah, Shri Abhay Poddar, Shri Roy Messay, Ms. sara Wong, Shri Naveen Munjal, Shri Ashok Singh, Shri Rajeev Rao and Ms. Christina at CL P power India Ltd

- ❖ Shri Ramesh Jatia, Shri N C Mehta, Shri K M Pai, Shri S R Vyas, Shri A N Rangaswamy, Shri Rajshekar, Shri Gaurang Zala at Bell Ceramics

- ❖ Shri Hemant Modi, Shri Suhas Joshi and Shri M A Baraiya at JMC Projects (I) Ltd

- ❖ Shri Rajubhai Gogri, Shri Kiritbhai Mehta, Shri Renil Gogri and Shri Rashesh gogari and Shri Mirik Gogri at Aarti Industries Ltd

- ❖ Shri Kanubhai Patel, Shri Brijesh Patel and Shri Mrunal Patel at Montecarlo Ltd

- ❖ Shri Pravinbhai Patel, Shri Arvind bhai Patel, Shri Krunalbhai and Shri Parth Patel at Patel Infrastructure Ltd

- ❖ Shri Rajubhai Agrawal, Shri Ronak and Shri Rohan Agrawal at N R Agarwal Industries Ltd

❖ Shri Kamlesh bhai shah, Shri Siddharthbhai and Shri Parth shah at RKC Infrabuilt Private Ltd

*****

8 : A Kaleidoscope of milestones

8.1   Accolades

Innovation in HR – 2018

**<u>Best Employee Engagement Professional of the year –
18th April 2018</u>**

<u>Best CHRO Award – 15th December 2018</u>

101 HR Super Achiever -2018

Excellence in HR Leadership Award - 16th October 2019

Best HR Mentor – 12th June 2019

HR Icon of the Year - 2019

Asia's 100 Power Leaders in Human Resources - 2022

HR Leader of the Year Award – 2022

GOLDEN AIM AWARDS
DYNERGIC Business Solution
Presents
GOLDEN AIM AWARDS
For Excellence & Leadership
18th February, 2023
ICONIC HR LEADERSHIP AWARD
Presented to
Dr. Jignesh Shah
Chief Human Resource Officer
RKC Infrabuilt Pvt Ltd
DIGITAL PARTNER
ASSOCIATE PARTNER
DigiOne+
FAMA
ICONIC HR LEADERSHIP AWARD
DR. JIGNESH SHAH
CHIEF HUMAN RESOURCE OFFICER
RKC INFRABUILT PVT LTD
GOLDEN AIM AWARDS is one of the most prestigious awards that recognize and rewards excellence & Leadership in the HR . The GOLDEN AIM Awards have been instituted by FEDERATION OF QUALITY EDU. COUNCIL to celebrate the achievements of respective professionals that have contributed immensely towards the growth of the respective industry.
Jury have undertaken below mentioned criteria to select Dr. Jignesh Shah profile for the award (Felicitation) :
• Innovative and Exemplary Practices
• Social Mobility
• Ability to Motivate and Inspire
• Strategic Innovation
• Integrity and Ethics
• Innovative HR Initiative
• Specific contribution under the Respective Segment

101 Top HR Minds

8.2 Certifications

STUDYGITA
Course Completion Certificate
THIS CERTIFICATE IS AWARDED TO
jigneshshah
FOR SUCCESSFULLY COMPLETING THE INDEPTH COURSE ON BHAGAVAD GITA, THE 'GITA MASTERY COURSE' DATED
September 27, 2022
WE APPRECIATE THE SINCERITY, DEDICATION AND DEVOTION.
Sumithra Krishna Das
TEMPLE PRESIDENT
Amarendr Gaur Das
Sukirti Madhavi DD
COURSE FACILITATORS
INTERNATIONAL SOCIETY FOR KRISHNA CONSCIOUSNESS (ISKCON)
Founder acharya : A.C. Bhaktivedanta Swami Srila prabhupada

CERTIFICATE OF COMPLETION
This is to certify that
jigneshshah
has successfully completed "Discover Yourself" course,
November 19, 2022
Sumithra Krishna Das
TEMPLE PRESIDENT
Adbhut Gopal Das
COURSE FACILITATORS
ISKCON CHENNAI
INTERNATIONAL SOCIETY FOR KRISHNA CONSCIOUSNESS
FOUNDER ACHARYA - A.C. BHAKTIVEDANTA SWAMI SRILA PRABHUPADA
WWW.ISKCONCHENNAI.ORG | WWW.STUDYGITA.COM
STUDYGITA

International Society for Krishna Consciousness (ISKCON)
FOUNDER ACHARYA - A.C. BHAKTIVEDANTA SWAMI SRILA PRABHUPADA
CERTIFICATE
OF COMPLETION
This is to Certify that
jigneshshah
has successfully completed the 'DEVOTION IN ACTION' Course
January 3, 2023
Sumithra Krishna Das
Temple President
Amarendr Gaur Das &
Sukirti Madhavi Devi Dasi
Course Facilitators
STUDYGITA
WWW.ISKCONCHENNAI.ORG | WWW.STUDYGITA.COM

Certificate of Completion
THIS IS TO CERTIFY THAT
jigneshshah
has successfully completed the 18-days "GITA MADE EASY"
May 28, 2023
Sumithra Krishna Das
TEMPLE PRESIDENT
Amarendr Gaur Das &
Sukirti Madhavi Devi Dasi
COURSE FACILITATORS
INTERNATIONAL SOCIETY FOR KRISHNA CONSCIOUSNESS
FOUNDER ACHARYA - A.C. BHAKTIVEDANTA SWAMI SRILA PRABHUPADA
WWW.ISKCONCHENNAI.ORG | WWW.STUDYGITA.COM

Reg No: YAI/IND/GJ/04RGJ5/2101/02

YOGA ALLIANCE INTERNATIONAL

CELEBRATE YOGA AND WELLNESS FOUNDATION

hereby certifies

Dr. Jignesh Shah

as a

YOGA TEACHER - MULTISTYLE

having completed all requirements of 300-hour Level training
and having demonstrated proficiency in Anatomy, Pranayama,
Meditation, Core Hatha Yoga Asanas, Yoga Philosophy &
Communication Skills.

15th June 2020 - 22nd December 2020

Rakeshgiri Goswami
Grandmaster of Yoga
Yoga Alliance International

Swami Vidyanand
Founder | President
Yoga Alliance International

K.M.Chandrashekaran
Organising Director
Yoga Alliance International

K.M Chandrashekaran

આદર્શ અમદાવાદ

"નેહલ", જૈન ઉપાશ્રયની બાજુમાં, કોમર્સ કોલેજ છ રસ્તા પાસે, નવરંગપુરા, અમદાવાદ-૩૮૦ ૦૦૯
ફોન નં. 2656 5416, 90330 15254
E-mail : aadarshamdavad@yahoo.co.in   Website : www.aadarshamdavad.org

પ્રમાણપત્ર

આદર્શ અમદાવાદ દ્વારા આયોજિત "બેઝીક ફેમીલી કાઉન્સેલર" ની તાલીમ ૧૫–૧૧–૨૦૧૯ થી ૨૪–૧–૨૦૨૦

સુધીમાં શ્રી/સુશ્રી _____ **Dr. Jignesh Shah** _____ સહભાગી બન્યા છે. તાલીમમાં સહભાગીને

ફેમીલી કાઉન્સેલર તરીકે કાર્ય કરવા જરૂરી જ્ઞાન, વલણો અને કુશળતાઓ પ્રાપ્ત કરવાની તક મળી છે, જેનાથી

તેઓ પોતે સક્ષમ બન્યા છે અને સમાજને સ્વૈચ્છિક રીતે ઉપયોગી થવામાં આ તાલીમનો ઉપયોગ કરશે તે હેતુ માટે

આ પ્રમાણપત્ર આપવામાં આવે છે.

સ્થળ : અમદાવાદ

તારીખ : ૨૪–૦૧–૨૦૨૦

ભરતભાઈ જે. શાહ
મેનેજીંગ ટ્રસ્ટી,
આદર્શ અમદાવાદ

M/s MonteCarlo Ltd.

Date: 30.09.2021

CERTIFICATE

This is to certify that **Dr. Jignesh Shah** had worked with us from 01.07.2017 to 30.09.2021 in the role of **HOD** as **Vice President- HR and Admin**.

During his association with us, we found him excellent in creating policies pertaining to HR & Admin function and execution of all policies and processes meticulously.

He is excellent in Talent Management and has executed many campus hiring activities during his tenure. He has established Learning & Development function and contributed in nurturing and maintaining learning culture in the Organisation.

Besides this, he is passionate about his work, result oriented coupled with excellent time management skill, high degree of commitment and standards of discipline.

He is sincere, meticulous, empathetic and thoughtful leader.

We wish him all the success for his future endeavour.

For **Montecarlo Limited,**

Brijesh Patel
Joint Managing Director

Montecarlo Limited
Montecarlo House

JMC Projects (India) Ltd.

ENGINEERS & CONSTRUCTORS
Regd & Corp Office A-104, Shapath 4, Opp Karnavati Club, S G Road, Ahmedabad-380 015 INDIA
Phone : +91-79-30011500 • Fax : +91-79-30011600, 30011700
E Mail : jmcho@jmcprojects.com • Web : www.jmcprojects.com

Date: 25/7/12

TO WHOMSOEVER IT MAY CONCERN

This is to certify that Mr. Jignesh Shah has been working with us since 9th Sept-2010 as Assistant Vice President (HR) heading our HR department.

During his association with us, we found him sincere, hard working and highly disciplined in his area of work. His contribution towards improving HR processes, putting the system in place and various HR initiatives are outstanding.

His proactive approach and timely response to the issues is a matter of pride.

On his own accord, he resigned from the services of the company.

We wish him all the success in his new assignments.

Regards,

M. A. Baraiya
Dy. President- HR & Admn

Committed to time & quality.

JMC Projects (India) Ltd.

ENGINEERS & CONSTRUCTORS
Regd & Corp. Office : A-104, Shapath-4, Opp. Karnavati Club, S. G. Road, Ahmedabad-380 051. INDIA
Phone : +91-79-30011500 • Fax : +91-79-30011600, 30011700
E.Mail : hmodi@jmcprojects.com • Web : www.jmcprojects.com

HEMANT MODI M S
Vice Chairman & Managing Director

28th July 2012

TO WHOMSOEVER IT MAY CONCERN

This is to certify that **Mr. Jignesh Shah** who has been working with us since 9th Sept-2010 as **Assistant Vice President (HR)** heading our HR department.

During his association with us, we found him innovative, sincere and hard working in his area of work. His contribution towards improving HR processes, putting the system in place and various HR initiatives are outstanding.

His proactive approach and timely response to the issues is a matter of pride.

On his own accord, he resigned from the services of the company.

We wish him all the success in his new assignments.

Regards,

HEMANT MODI

TO WHOMSOEVER IT MAY CONCERN

This is to certify that Dr. Jignesh Shah had worked with us from 10th May,2022 to 10th October,2022 in the capacity of Vice President-HR/Admn heading our HR/Admn department based at Corporate office, Baroda.

During his association, we found him excellent in all our recruitment activities, Employees engagement initiatives, HR Operations, HR Policy formation, Performance appraisal and all other HR Processes.

He had demonstrated high qualities of Leadership, result oriented approach, passionate for his work and time management skill.

He decided to part with us due to his compelling personal and family reasons. We respected his decision and with heavy heart, we relieved him.

We wish him all the success in his future endeavor and best wishes to overcome his personal and family reasons.

With Good Luck,

(Parth Patel)

Director- Commercial

Date: 10/10/22

Date: 22nd March, 2010

<u>TO WHOMSO EVER IT MAY CONCERN</u>

This is to certify that Mr Jignesh Shah- DGM (HR & Admn.) has been working with us since 12th Sept, 2005 with CLP-India. During his association with us, we found him innovative, sincere and hardworking in his area of work. His contribution towards improving statutory compliance, establishing Contract Management system, liaison with Government agencies and community, HR initiatives etc are noteworthy.

He also made an excellent contribution in sourcing the manpower in time. His proactive approach and timely response to the issues is a matter of pride.

On his own accord, he resigned from the services of the company.

We wish him all the success in his new assignments.

Anup Kundu
Construction Project Director

M/s Bell Ceramics Ltd.

10 SEP 2005

<u>To whomsoever it may concern</u>

Mr Jignesh Shah has been with us for nearly 5 years, initially as Sr Manager and later as Asst General Manager – HR.

Mr Shah is knowledgeable and keeps himself abreast of latest trends in the field. He has handled HR, IR, Training and General Administration very efficiently. He also has conducted several inhouse training programs on soft skills.

Overall he has made a significant contribution in shaping and modernising the HR philosophy of the company in a changing environment.

Mr Jignesh Shah is leaving our organization to pursue higher career goals. We wish him every success in his future endeavours.

K M Pai
Chief Executive Officer

Corporate Office 'Panorama', 3rd Floor, R.C. Dutt Road, Vadodara - 390 007 Gujarat (India)
Tel : +91-265-2335844, 2331384 Fax : +91-265-2336490 E-mail : info@bellceramic.com

07/09/2005

TO WHOMSOEVER IT MAY CONCERN

This is to certify that Mr. Jignesh Shah has been working with us since 1st March 2001, presently designated as "Assistant General Manager (HR)", heading our HR Department.

During his tenure with us, Mr. Shah had contributed exemplary towards HR related issues and shown the qualities of excellent leadership. We also found him innovative and pro-active in dealing with issues related to people. He possesses commitment, dedication & innovative ideas and worked with us with utmost sincerity. He has excellent communication skills which generates human touch to employees.

Mr. Shah, on his own decided to leave us. We feel it is a loss to the organization. We regret to relieve him after office hours of 10th September 2005.

We wish him all the success in his exemplary career and growth in the field of HR.

For Bell Ceramics Limited,

Ramesh Jatia
Managing Director

www.bellceramic.com

Corporate Office: Panorama, 3rd Floor, R.C. Dutt Road, Vadodara - 390 007 Gujarat (India)
Tel: +91-265-2335844, 2331384 Fax: +91-265-2336490 E-mail: info@bellceramic.com
Regd. Office (Dora Works): Village: Dora, Taluka: Amod, District: Bharuch - 392 230, Gujarat (India) Tel: +91-2641-235151, 235153 Fax: +91-2641-235160

TO WHOMSOEVER IT MAY CONCERN

This is to certify that Mr.Jignesh Shah has been working with us since 1ˢᵗ March, 2001 currently designated as **AGM (HR)** heading our **HR Dept.**

During his association with us, we found him extremely sensitive, empathetic and live to the needs of human beings and solve their problems with passion and missionary zeal. As a responsible change agent, he has helped the Management in various HR initiatives for the development of people in and around the industry.

He has earned a good name for his openness and transparent behaviour in dealing with people in distress. He keeps himself abreast with the latest trends/ happenings in his profession and allied subjects and is always eager to learn new things. His interpersonal relationships with every one, he comes in contact with is commendable. He has many qualities of head and heart.

Mr. Shah on his own decided to leave us. We regret to relieve him after office hours of 10ᵗʰ September, 2005.

We wish him Good Luck for his future assignment.

With Best Wishes,

S.R. VYAS
Sr.V.P. (CA)

DATE   : 08.09.2005
PLACE : DORA

www.bellceramic.com

Corporate Office : Panorama, 3rd Floor, R.C. Dutt Road, Vadodara - 390 007 Gujarat (India)
Tel. : +91 265 2335844, 2331384 Fax : +91 265 2336490 E-mail : info@bellceramic.com

M/s Reliance Industries Ltd.

Reliance
Industries Limited

Village-Mora, Post-Bhatha, Surat-Hazira Road, Dist. Surat (Gujarat), PIN : 394 510
Tel. : 860401 to 860410. Telex : 0188-447 RPL IN. Telefax : 0261-895229, 895189, 895209

27th Feb. 2001

TO WHOMSOEVER IT MAY CONCERN

This is to certify that **Mr. Jignesh Shah, Dy. Manager – HRSS** has been developed as an excellent trainer.

During his tenure with us, he conducted various training programmes for different category of employees on various HR related topics and these were well received by participants through structured feedback.

Mr. Shah has been very sincere, committed and devoted person towards training activities.

We wish him all the success in his new assignments.

S K Minocha
General Manager (MPD)

Regd. Office : Maker Chambers IV, 3rd Floor, 222, Nariman Point, Mumbai 400 021, India.

Reliance
Industries Limited

Village-Mora, Post-Bhatha, Surat-Hazira Road, Dist. Surat (Gujarat), PIN : 394 510
Tel. : 860401 to 410. Telefax : 0261 - 725229, 725189, 725209

27/2/2001

TO WHOMSOEVER IT MAY CONCERN

This is to certify that Mr. Jignesh Shah has been working with us as Dy. Manager (HRSS) since 1st March 1996. During his association with us Mr. Shah contributed significantly in maintaining cordial Industrial Relations in the Organisation. He possesses commitment, dedication & innovative ideas & worked with us with utmost sincerity. He has excellent communication skills which generates human touch to employees.

Mr. Shah on his own decided to leave us. We feel it is a loss to the Organisation. We regret to relieve him after office hours of 28th February 2001.

We wish him all the success in his exemplary career and growth in the field of HR.

Good Luck.

FOR RELIANCE INDUSTRIES LIMITED

(N.K. GAUR)
VICE PRESIDENT (HRSS)

Regd. Office : Maker Chambers IV, 3rd Floor, 222, Nariman Point, Mumbai 400 021, India.

28th February, 1996

<u>TO WHOMSOEVER IT MAY CONCERN</u>

This is to certify that Mr. Jignesh R. Shah has been working with us since 15th October, 1990 in Personnel Department, presently designated as Personnel Executive. During his association with us, he was responsible for disciplinary matters, Court matters, all IR issues, Training and developmental activities and Recruitment assignments.

During his tenure of services with us we found him hardworking, sincere and having professional abilities to handle the various issues.

He has decided to leave us on his own accord. With a regret, we relieve him w.e.f. 28.02.96. We wish him all success in his career.

For LUPIN LABORATORIES LTD.

N.B. VADIA
WORKS MANAGER

Feedback

Please write to us for your feedback/comments to:

Dr Jignesh Shah

Email: Jignesh.shah1964@gmail.com

LinkedIn:

https://www.linkedin.com/in/dr-jignesh-shah-7656b21b/

Facebook:

https://www.facebook.com/profile.php?id=100094556809044

Mobile number: +91 9824275610

*****

www.ingramcontent.com/pod-product-compliance
Lightning Source LLC
LaVergne TN
LVHW012137060726
842759LV00027B/668